THE ART
OF
THE DOG

by

THOMAS
PURCELL

NEW YORK
THANE & PROSE
2016

First Edition

Book cover and book interior design by Jerry Holthouse

ISBN 978-0-9970795-9-3

Cataloging-in-Publication Data is available from
The Library of Congress
Printed in The United States

THANE
&
PROSE

I wish to dedicate this work, first and foremost,
to all of my professors—every last four legged one of them.

I would also like to dedicate this work to my Sal
without whom you would probably be reading gibberish.

To Jake and Melissa who continue to prove you can achieve greatness
by shooting for the moon and being happy where you land.

To Liv and Chance who are my true loves.

And, to Justa Goodell, the person who trusted me,
gave me a chance and taught me every bit as much as I hope I have taught her.

And finally, to Zeke and Thane for seeing something,
having faith—and going with it!

Renee & Stephanie

Enjoy the read

and thank for support

I love Bassett~

THE ART
OF
THE DOG

THE ART OF THE DOG

1
The Why of It

2
The Red Leash

3
Qigong, The Language of Energy

4
Inquiring Minds

5
Spanky the Ghost Hunter

6
"She's Mine, I Tell You"

7
The Yorkie with the Fifty-Five Gallon Bladder

8
The Incidental Experiment

9
Bailey versus the Tea Kettle—and Every Other Noise

10
Bear and Food Aggression

11
Star's Troubles in the Barn

12
The Kindness of Strangers

13
Your Turn?

To My Readers,

The reason I felt compelled to write this book?
I guess I am a bit of a rebel in that I disagree with much of the practices I
see from many other dog trainers. Having established that, I don't claim
to be the know all and end all of dog training. What I do believe is that if
you follow the information that I am sharing, you should have the joy of a
great relationship with your K9 best friend.

1

THE WHY
OF IT

I have often been referred to as a dog whisperer.

Although I'm sure this sobriquet is intended to be complimentary, I have never been comfortable with it. A dog whisperer gets into the psychology of dog behavior, using methods and techniques to correct a misguided, confused, or misbehaving dog. This practice is fantastic in many ways—but a dog whisperer I am unequivocally not.

Instead, I'm glad I was blessed to have been initially influenced by the best: my first ever dog training professor—my mom.

Mom was a hazel-eyed, white-haired, tough Irish woman who raised seven children with an "I have an iron fist, a strong will, and I'll do what it takes to get things done" attitude. My dad, a hard-working, intimidating Irishman with thinning hair and smiling eyes, always brought home the new family dog, but it was always Mom's magic creating the amazing pets they became. She always uniquely understood mutts. Not one of our family pets ever came from a breeder. Not a single penny was spent acquiring these dogs. Their lives generally started in a barn and ended up at our house in the center of the city, in a neighborhood of so many houses so close together, you could borrow a cup of sugar through the window without ever leaving the comfort of your kitchen.

I learned when quite young to gaze into a dog's soul. I know it's said now that dogs don't have souls, but you will never convince me there is no spiritual energy at work. Why do you think the word dog is a transposition of the word God?

Further training came from loving and knowing my own dogs. Recently, someone asked if I would dedicate this book to these special animals, well, it is: to my dogs, past and present. People also often remark about the way they seem to be a bit unnaturally attached to me; I could never disagree, but I have always attributed this to the power of the alpha and to the two-way trust.

Indeed, these dogs have taught me so much—dogs such as Midnight, our family's first one, a black Labrador Retriever. My father came home one day and dropped this eight week old Labrador retriever at my mother's feet, a gift from one of his farmer friends. Midnight became our newest family member!

Labrador Retrievers are by nature swimmers, bred by Canadian fishermen to assist with fetching fish and with retrieving nets. Midnight was no exception. As kids, my parents would take us all to our summer home at the lake, a quaint cottage without the luxury of running water; needless to say, we thought we were rich. My brothers, sisters, and I used to pretend that we were drowning; reflecting back, I can see how sophomoric that was; nevertheless, Midnight, every time without hesitation, would save us. We grabbed her tail, and she swam us to shore. We called her our lifeguard. But we were ignorant, young and eager and kept this up until we realized that we had overdone it. Midnight got sick. Luckily she healed. In hindsight, we probably nearly drowned her.

Another example of our childhood ignorance, pertaining to dogs of course: in the city there was a plethora of abandoned industrial buildings, begging to be investigated, and we always took Midnight with us on these adventures. On one of our trips to an old cement factory, we were walking down one of the dark, damp hallways when Midnight cried out: she had badly cut her ankle. It was bleeding so profusely, we feared we would lose her right there. We knew we had to get her home fast, and we trotted ten blocks home, keeping pressure on the wound but fearing the worst. When we rushed into the house with her, Mom told us to tightly wrap the wound and to keep a close eye on her ourselves: supporting seven kids made affording a vet impossible. Midnight healed within a few short weeks, but my brother and I caught hell for what had happened. In retrospect, I ask myself, "Who takes a dog into an abandoned industrial building?"

Midnight lived to be fifteen years old, dying when I was seventeen. She had shared my entire childhood. We'd grown so close through the years that, while I was away on a camping trip, a strange feeling came over me. I knew Midnight was in good health but was unable to help feeling that something was wrong. It was a gnawing sensation. I shared my fears with my brother Dan, who simply insulted me and questioned my intellect, as well as my overall mental well being. When I got home, I threw open the large front door and immediately asked Mom where Midnight was. She told me Midnight had died. No surprise. Somehow, I had just known! Mom told me that while I was away, Midnight had become so sick that Dad had carried her to the basement and held her until she passed away. My dad, the strong, tough, World War II Marine Corp veteran of the South Pacific, had cried hard that night.

Shortly after losing Midnight, we were again at the lake when neighbors across the street told us their dog had birthed Pointer mix puppies, one of which became the family dog between our Labrador Retrievers. She was six weeks old, white with random black markings. The runt of the litter, she grew to only twenty pounds—not much for a Pointer. We named her Cookie.

Cookie was a poor bird dog, and by no means is that an insult; just a fact. But, she was everything we wanted in a family dog. She loved nothing more than to clown around, climb ladders, jump through hoops, and run around like one of us. I remember lying on my back on the living room floor, watching television. My head and hands rested against the base of the couch when, suddenly, I felt a small paw dart from underneath the couch and sit on my hand. I remember thinking, "This is just too cute." That gives you an idea just how small Cookie was. Sadly, this was my last memory of Cookie, who went hunting with Dad and Dan the next morning and never returned. They thought Cookie had gotten lost. For days afterward, Dad returned to the hunting fields to find her. He never did. We concluded that someone had stolen her.

Two years after losing Cookie, my girlfriend at the time, gave me a black Labrador Retriever, an eight week old, brown-eyed fur ball. I had this puppy for about an hour, until Mom persuaded me that Dad needed another dog and that because it was his birthday, I should give him the puppy. So, I put a yellow ribbon around her neck, went to Dad, and said, "What's black and yellow and just what you need?" I put the puppy in his arms, and she became his. He named her Middy, after Midnight.

Middy loved all the time and became Dad's best friend, going everywhere with him. He took her hunting and fishing. They were quite a pair. She was entirely selfless and full of affection, so much so that the entire neighborhood claimed her for their own. Occasionally she would go missing; we feared that she'd become lost, but there she was at one of those neighbors' homes behaving as though she lived there. When she died fifteen years later, she departed in first class canine style: she left one winter evening and never returned. Come spring, we found her under a pine tree in melting snow, realizing she'd died the way she'd lived, loving and putting everyone else's feelings first.

A few years after gifting Middy to Dad, I married and fathered two children. When it was time for a family dog, I made a beeline to the local animal shelter. Strolling among the many kennels, my eye caught a beautiful orange-and-white Brittany Spaniel/Collie mix who spotted me and worked her way to the front of the cage. After spending time with her, I asked the attendant to hold this dog for a few hours. I went home, picked up my six-year-old daughter Melissa, and returned to the shelter. Without pointing out any particular dog, I asked Melissa which dog she liked most. She gravitated immediately toward the same Brittany/Collie mix I had selected. Done! We had a new family member. Melissa and I named her Kelly even before arriving home; it must have been Kelly's vermillion hair. The shelter had believed her to be about two years old. She was a great family dog who diligently guarded our house and family members. She was my sweet best friend, and several years later I got Kelly in the divorce.

Kelly was mild-mannered and sweet but a bit of a wanderer. After the divorce, I purchased a "project" house in the country, one that needed rebuilding as much as I did. While my close friend Keith and I worked on the house, Kelly roamed the surrounding fields. She loved the country. One day, I watched Kelly sitting on the side of the road, watching oncoming cars, and when the traffic cleared, she shot across the street for more fields to explore. She was a dog so easygoing, that everyone was shocked about her fiercely protective nature—the ferocious side. One night around two A.M., I awoke to growling and barking. I found Kelly with her teeth around the ankle of one of the would-be-thieves trying to steal Keith's ladders and scaffolding he'd left at my house for the remodeling. He was so grateful, he kept Kelly supplied with a lifetime of treats. My mouse had roared like a lion that night!

But Kelly feared thunderstorms. During one storm, she cowered in the garage and we discovered she had scratched the entire side of the car desperately trying to crawl inside for refuge. Afterwards, we kept her safely in the house. She lived to be twelve years old. It became increasingly difficult for her to walk and to see and, unfortunately, I lived in a cookie cutter neighborhood where every house looked the same. The neighborhood kids often had to bring her home to show her where her house was. Soon thereafter, I took her to the vet for evaluation, who determined it was time to let her go.

Their whole lives, our dogs depend on us to do the right thing for them, and one of these duties includes an acutely painful final decision.

Many years later, I acquired Sasha, a Doberman Pinscher, three years old and already trained, with cropped ears and tail and with perfect Doberman markings. She was all muscle, and became my final partner in the police department. And for the record? This policeman never felt safer than when Sasha was by my side.

Once, there was this assault attempt; I was about to get jumped. But before he even got close? Sasha was leaping through the air, exposing teeth heading straight for his neck. Inches before contact, I called her off, and she dropped to the ground. I was always amazed by her level of obedience and by her extensive vocabulary. This guy had no idea how narrowly he had escaped being severely injured. I never had a better friend than Sasha. On the job, she would have given her life for me; as a friend, she was sheer beauty.

Another time, I headed to Montana for a couple of weeks, and a friend reminded me I should tell Sasha I was leaving for a while. She looked me right in the eyes, turned the other way, and gave me the cold shoulder. After I stopped laughing, I could not believe she'd actually understood me. I coaxed her back to face me and repeated, "Sasha, I have to go to Montana and will be back in a few weeks." Again, she stood up and turned her back to me.

I wound up taking her with me.

Some of my best times were with Sasha during my frequent visits to the lake. We headed to the lake even in the winter months. There were times when it was so cold—Sasha slept on the couch with me solely to share body heat. We were that inseparable.

Sasha was yet another case of loving her until she was too old to see or walk, and in the months before her death she was in great pain. Again, I was faced with the difficult, responsible decision to do the right thing by my dog. I sat in the room with her at the vet's office, and when it was time, Sasha actually handed her paw to the vet, her brown eyes gazing up at me with tender gratitude.

I held her while she exhaled her last.

There were no dogs in my life for years after Sasha. There were so many things going on in my life: the marriage of my daughter, the arrival of my new granddaughter, my own new marriage, and the building of my new house. Then some good friends decided I had mourned and had been dogless long enough. When their three-year-old, silver Weimaraner had puppies, they insisted I had to have one of them. On July 3rd, a popular night for celebrating Independence Day in my area, they dropped off one of the four week olds named Carley (they'd even named her for me). We got her at four weeks because her mother had stopped feeding her and her siblings by then.

My initial reluctance turned into gratitude. Carley turned out to be the most talented bird hunter I had ever owned. Our ability to communicate was beyond incredible. It also bears mentioning that throughout my time with her, I also fostered many other dogs. Carley was always the balanced dog keeping me safe and the visiting dogs stable. We were great partners.

And then came Luke. While you will read all about Luke farther into this book, I must establish now that he was a curious addition to our family indeed. You see, I understood Luke—and I understood Luke in a unique way.

While I explain my history with dogs, it seems only appropriate I explain why I feel such an instinctive connection with them. Growing up, I was in the middle of seven children. Every middle child can attest that we are the most sensitive. Being a bit challenged with dyslexia didn't make things any easier; in the 1950's and 1960's no one knew much about dyslexia. I remember being told by Sister Mary Claire, my teacher at the time, that I was just a daydreamer.

Overall, I was a fairly happy kid growing up. But, again, being the middle of seven, I was often lost in the sauce. An example, an unsurprising one, is that there are no baby or toddler photographs of me in the now old and yellowed family albums. My older brother and I were twenty-one months apart, but we were raised quite differently. I have always enjoyed telling the anecdote of how differently we grew up and why.

My brother Dan was regarded as academically brilliant, a sharp student in Catholic elementary school who graduated with honors. The problem was, he wanted to attend a public high school with his friends. My parents said, "No, you're going to Archbishop Turner, the private Catholic school." When I graduated from elementary school, after repeating eighth grade, I asked my parents if I was going to Archbishop Turner as well, and they said, "No, you're going to the vocational high school where you'll learn a trade, even if it's only to learn how to make license plates."

When my brother graduated from high school, he got a summer job landscaping in a cemetery. He loved the job. Dan explained this to my parents and told them he wanted to forego college. My parents responded, "No, you're going to college for a degree." When I graduated from high school, I asked my parents, "Hey Mom, Dad, what college am I going to?" Of course, their answer was, "You're going into the military."

It may be hard to believe this story can possibly correlate to my world of dogs, but it does. I always preach direction. My parents realized my brother and I needed direction; no choices—individualized direction.

How does all this struggle, sensitivity, insight, and survival create the capability to read dogs? By creating recognition of a lack of respect: I believe there is no species in the entire world who suffer from a lack of respect more than fish—and dogs.

First, the fish. A hooked fish is treated like a creature with no feelings at all, violently jerked from the water to asphyxiate and to be butchered while still alive. Brutal, but you never hear anyone complain about the life, or death, of a fish.

And then there is the dog. A dog can sustain starvation, beatings, neglect—and what does it do? It responds with unconditional love. The only reason for biting is fear. And we think everything will be okay if we offer a treat.

The crazy thing? Dogs will forgive it all over a simple treat.

I have always found myself amazed that I am able to recognize levels of fear in dogs, more than most other people. This doesn't mean I feel sorry for the dogs; it simply means I understand them. I understand the difficult place they may find themselves in. I understand the frustration and the weariness. Thus, the reasons for my seeming insight into the behavior of dogs—but let's move into training mode.

Again, dogs will forgive for a treat. But treats are for tricks—not for discipline. You don't give a dog a treat because it came when you called him or sat when you asked him to. Commands are too important to a dog/master relationship to be distracted by, or minimized by, treats. My treat rule? Treats are fun, optional, whereas obedience is necessary, not optional.

The three commands are come, sit, and stay. "Come" is the most important command, particularly for the safety of the animal. "Sit" is great because it takes the dog out of play mode and into a neutral position. But the most powerful command is the "Stay" position, especially the long stay, teaching the dog patience and also sending the strong message that you are the alpha, the one in charge.

Now, let's talk about the alpha.

This is how alpha works: alpha wolf is not a position that some dog is driven to by his ego. It happens because he has no choice. If the pack is to survive and he is the strongest member, then it's in his DNA to step up and dominate the pack. It's a tough position to hold with a ton of responsibility that I bet he would rather never assume, but again, there is no choice.

It is this act of nature, alpha position, which gets a lot of our pets into trouble. If a dog lives in a household where he perceives weakness, he may attempt to take over; in other words, he believes that he is alpha to his human pack.

When I go into a home and find this is the problem, I sit the family down and explain that dogs love affection—but don't need it. Many clients take exception to this opening statement until I fully explain; at this point I see eyes open and jaws drop. I explain further that alpha wolf does not show affection; he bestows direction. Here is the formula for success: when you give a dog direction, he feels secure; when a dog feels secure, he also feels safe; and when he feels safe, he is happy; and when he is happy, all your problems seem to go away. Easy, simple, and true. Invariably, I seem to find an alpha dog running the show with his human pack, and there's the problem: it's not ideal.

I recently encountered a beautiful family that had rescued a Husky/Shepherd from the local shelter. You could not have met a sweeter family unit or a nicer canine. The family comprised a mom and dad and three extremely high-energy kids. The chaos during my visit was unbelievable. Their dog Apollo was not only large (eighty-plus pounds) but also out of control. That combination meant someone was accidently going to get hurt. All Apollo was doing was his utmost to control the confusion because he perceived this energy as a weakness.

When I arrived at the home, Apollo greeted me outside. He was calm but appeared exhausted; he had little idea who I was but seemed desperate to understand. I generally spend my first ten minutes with a dog establishing myself as an alpha character, but not this time. We just sat quietly on the front porch without words. I needed Apollo to feel a sense of calmness and peace. I don't remember ever having a dog stare at me in such a way: soft, peaceful, but fatigued. His shoulders appeared to slump a little in clear weariness. For maybe half an hour, we just sat, enjoying the summer day, watching traffic and listening to the leafy neighborhood of other dogs and children.

Suddenly, Apollo's family arrived home, and crazy came with them. Within minutes, the environment turned from calm and serene to loud and chaotic. Two of the children began arguing; one child was standing in the yard crying and pulling at Apollo's collar trying to move him. Still, while all of this transpired, I saw in Apollo's eyes love and concern for his family. At that moment, I realized what I could do for Apollo, and that was to teach his family what they could do for him. I would clarify for them what was making him anxious, destructive, and causing him to act out. I would show them how to improve the situation with their actions. In short, I would educate the family in the alpha philosophy. What I found most intriguing about this visit was that Apollo was a truly upbeat dog who loved his pack and merely needed someone to give him direction, someone to simply make him feel safe.

2
THE RED LEASH

The red leash concept came to me so simply, I feel I can hardly take any credit for it. An inexpensive lead just happened to be what the local animal shelter, where I volunteer, had always used, and it also just happened to have been red. I had no idea it was going to be such a perfect tool. But I found the results from using this tool were immediate; and when using it properly, the dog almost automatically began making eye contact with me, looking up at me for information and direction. It has been the perfect gateway for communication and, subsequently, success. To be honest, it was the perfect accident.

It's quite simple: a red nylon twine with a large loop on one end and a tiny loop on the opposite end. I feed the larger loop through the smaller loop, forming an adjustable loop that will fit the neck of any size dog. The original large loop is then slipped onto my right wrist. There is no hardware in this leash at all. It is my opinion that any hardware such as a small ring or leash clip will impede the direct flow of energy, and having a direct conduit between you and the dog allows this direct flow of energy. Remember: energy flows both ways.

I never hold this leash in my hand because a quick pull from the dog would easily slip right off. If the loop is around my wrist, the dog remains under my control even if I trip, fall into a lake, or end up in a snow bank; I will still have my dog. The adjustable end of the leash is placed over your dog's head and high behind the ears. Humans and dogs both have sensitive pressure points behind their ears. When the red leash is in place, high behind the ears and over the pressure points, the dog is under total control. In most cases, the dog protests this new and uncomfortable feeling, but the protest lasts about thirty seconds, and then you have full cooperation.

I then walk my dog in the heeling position on my left side. Why the left side? It's mostly for continuity, but it was also designed to keep the right hand and arm free. The purpose of this is either for shaking hands or for the hunter to use his right side to carry and to shoot his weapon. In modern days, think of it as a way to keep the cell phone hand free.

If this high behind the ears technique sounds familiar, it is probably because this is what professionals use at dog shows; after all, presenting a dog in a show requires perfect control. When taking your own dog for a walk at home, this technique also keeps your dog's head up high and looking proud. Isn't it wonderful to imagine your dog walking down the street with you and the dog heeling proudly at your side, not pulling and not sniffing the ground? It's a pretty sight. Observers will compliment and appreciate the way you handle your pet.

When I teach my clients, I stress that, although I want them to walk their dog with the red leash, I don't want them to think of it as a walking leash, but rather as a training leash.

Eventually, when Fido sees the leash, he knows you mean business.

I would be remiss if I didn't state how I feel about harnesses and retractable leashes. I'm okay with a harness if you're having your dog pull a cart or a sleigh. Otherwise, a harness provides no true control over the dog. I have also often been told by users of the harness that the pet is more comfortable. While this may be true, it's important to remember what makes a dog happy is feeling secure. And without control of your dog, the dog isn't feeling secure.

Again, for a dog, security equals safe, and safe equals happy. Some people for the sake of convenience keep their dog outfitted with a harness 24/7. That is their prerogative, but I can't imagine anyone wanting to wear a bra 24 hours a day.

As for the retractable leash, it seems to me like a recipe for disaster, because you have no control over your dog when using one; when I ask people why they like them, they say it gives their dog the feeling of freedom to move around. Once more, freedom is not what your pet needs or wants; your pet wants and needs direction in order to feel secure.

If the red leash is in the proper position, high behind the ears, and Fido attempts to pull or get too far ahead, a light, quick snap of the leash with the left hand will yield a correction. It is also important to add a correction noise with the corrective snap. It's important to note that you don't want to merely pull on the leash—it needs to be a snap. If you only pull on the leash, the dog can pull back, and to a dog this is a game. If you snap the leash with your left hand, the dog cannot snap back, and now you have a correction. When I am teaching, I instruct my clients to watch my left hand. I use a fingertip control technique, gentle and relaxed, held with my left hand. If I need to give a correction, it is so subtle it may be difficult for the client to detect, but the dog will easily detect it; in fact, if I am relaxed, the dog is relaxed, if I am tense, the dog is tense. It's about energy, and your energy is always traveling through the red leash.

Use the red leash to lead your dog. You can either lead your dog to a response you desire or away from a situation you don't want. For example, I don't believe a dog should be able to climb on his favorite piece of furniture unless he is invited. If he is allowed to climb on the couch when he feels like it, he will claim that couch.

In his thinking, it is his and no longer belongs to you.

My rule is: until he starts paying the mortgage and the bills, nothing is his. When Fido helps himself to the couch or chair, grab that red leash and show it to him. If you don't get a reaction, place it on him and lead him off the couch. Don't ever push a dog. You should not push a dog any sooner than you should push a horse. If you push a horse, you're asking to get kicked; push a dog, and you may be bitten. Again, I don't have a problem with Fido on the furniture if you don't. After all, it is your furniture—but he should be invited.

With the red leash comes its power of suggestion, the mere sight of it by your dog can do wonders for you. Friends of mine rescued a terribly overweight, sullen, yellow Labrador Retriever from a local shelter. They named her Bella. Bella was a bit of a head case, and, unsurprisingly, she came from a bad situation—a puppy mill.

Imagine your entire life is spent being held captive in a small, cramped cage. You are fed but are never let out of your enclosure. You have become so obese that even the three inches of give between you and the bars holding you become threatened. You have never felt grass beneath your feet, and you never bark because you don't know how. You don't even know that it's wrong to eat your own feces. All you know is that you are to birth puppies, over and over again. This is your life. Once you are no longer able to produce the expected litters of puppies, you are discarded; if you're lucky, you are taken to an animal shelter, if that animal shelter will accept you. And if the shelter does accept you, you have yet another hurdle, finding a loving family to adopt you. If you are unlucky or never adopted, you may be euthanized.

This fate is a puppy mill's sickening offering to dogs.

When my friends, a sweet couple whose children were grown and independent, brought Bella home, she found a comfortable bed and a pile of furry toys to keep her company. Bella lay down on the bed, gathered all her toys closely to her as if they were her babies and gave me the impression she would never move again. This behavior posed a problem, because eventually Miss Bella would have to relieve herself, so we placed the red leash on her and led her outside to the unfamiliar plushness of green grass and initiated her education. Bella quickly discovered that grass is nice stuff to smell, to walk on, and, most importantly, to poop on. After one or two sessions of being led, or trained, with the red leash, all that my friends had to do was to show her that red leash and Bella was up and heading enthusiastically for the door to pee.

An interesting side story about Bella: she learned to heel almost instantly, but I expected a Labrador Retriever, a hunting dog, to be a bit more curious on walks. She lived in a densely rural setting loaded with lots of critters but never seemed to use her nose, probably because life in a cage has no need for olfactory senses. Poor Bella just had no idea how to be a dog. She had never barked, sniffed, or even run.

One day my friend and I put a pack of dogs together for a walk. This pack was formed by my own alumni whom I had trained, including our five-year-old chocolate Labrador Retriever also named Bella, my nine-year-old black Labrador Retriever/Weimaraner mix named Carley, and an intimidating six-year-old Blue Nose Pit Bull named Hammer. At a young age, Hammer's ears were cut off by the sinister people who use these breeds of dogs for fights. Mercifully, Hammer was rescued. And despite his poor history, Hammer is one of the most balanced dogs I have ever met.

We set off on a no leash pack walk through woods and fields. All the dogs had a great time running, noses working overtime in leaves and weeds after a fresh rainfall. They also simply explored one another. All of them except poor Bella, the Yellow Lab from the puppy mill. She simply would not leave our side. She had no idea how to behave, no idea how to explore or appreciate these rich surroundings. We decided to tie Bella to one end of a red leash and Hammer the Blue Nose Pit Bull to the other. When Hammer took off running as fast as his legs permitted, Bella had no choice but to take off with him; probably in such shock, she feared a heart attack. She had never run before but was suddenly and certainly thrust into learning how to. Before long, she was off the red leash, discovering and exploring all the new scents, hunting with the pack, happy as could be.

A full year elapsed before Bella become a real dog. She is now barking, running, and bonding with her owners—a vibrantly happy real dog! One last note about Bella: my friends did adopt a second dog from the shelter, a small but not young, gregarious Shih Tzu named Levi. Levi was a great contributor to Bella's healing. A second adoption can be a positive on an unbalanced dog, but only if the second dog is already solidly balanced.

One of the things I love to point out to people when they catch on to the proper use of the red leash while heeling their dog is how good it looks and how great it feels to walk your dog with pride. Trust me, people notice and comment on what they see. "Look how nice that dog walks, and look how it's not pulling." Everyone loves to look good no matter the activity; and when you're in control, walking the dog becomes fun.

For seven years, I was the house emcee at a nightclub at the Buffalo, New York downtown Hilton. I hosted every event from music festivals to fashion shows. One of my duties was to run the karaoke shows on Friday's Happy Hour. I always started the show by performing a song or two. I know for a fact that you really have to look good to feel good. On one of my show days I was running late, and though I started the show on time, I noticed I had a black shoe on my left foot and an unmatching brown shoe on my right. I joked and appeared to laugh it off, but I felt like an idiot. I did the show in my socks. My performance was not my best.

Another time I started a show with a difficult song and knocked it out of the park. As I left the stage, this well dressed, handsome black man came up to me and said he thought I was amazing, and asked whether I was singing or merely lip-synching? I assured him that was really me and thanked him most sincerely. Just as I was just starting to get full of myself, he stated, "Well man, you sound great and if you ever learn how to dress, you might really have it going on." I was crushed, and that exchange threw my performance off the rest of the night, but I had learned the importance of looking good.

I realize that stressing about how good you look may seem a bit shallow when we are stressing the importance of dog training, but I am only attempting to help you stay in the program and the right mindset. Feeling great about what you are accomplishing is aided by maintaining an image of looking good while you walk your dog. Taking pride in good form if you will. The walk, after all, is your bonding time with your dog. It's where your best friend learns to trust, depend, and acquire his levels of security. Remember however, Fido gets no choices; he is never ahead of you. Heeling means at your side.

Additionally, if you tense up when another dog approaches, your dog will also tense up. As you walk, if you are choking the dog, stop and make the necessary adjustments to the leash and begin again. But do relax; if you are tense, the dog will be tense; if you remain calm, your puppy will remain calm.

As the other dog approaches and you need to issue a correction, remember not to pull but to issue the same gentle but firm snap used earlier. If you pull, your dog's natural instinct is to pull back, interpreting the ruse for a game, and the fact that he is unable to snap back assures that the technique will be interpreted as a correction.

Remember, a secure dog is a happy dog, and the red leash will help you to accomplish just that.

3
QIGONG, THE LANGUAGE OF ENERGY

I had a dear friend who resided at one of the most beautiful, spiritual, and sacred places on earth: Lily Dale, New York. Lily Dale is near a college town northeast of Chautauqua Lake. It was established as Lily Dale Assembly in 1906. It is a serene little community tucked away from much of the bustle of the surrounding rural communities. With its lush greenery, it has always been a well-known home to many mediums, psychics, and spiritual advisors. Upon entering Lily Dale, there is an immediate sense of incredible energy and peace. I have known people who have entered the gates of Lily Dale only to immediately turn around; they just could not handle the intense sensations that came over them—a haunted feeling.

The most popular season for Lily Dale is summertime. At the gates of Lily Dale, you are greeted with amazing, pristinely designed gardens of lilies and many other tall, beautiful flowers and greenery. The lawns are well-manicured around a small, peaceful lake.

Within this charming, tight-knit community are many antiquated houses, suiting perfectly the landscape. Many of these homes are two-story with wooden railings and colorful wooden shutters. The porches glimmer with terra cotta pots brimming with colorful flowers and baskets hanging from the floor of the overhead deck. Some of these homes nestle in clusters, and others are farther away from the lake and the immediate community setting. Each home is decorated according to the unique taste of the particular resident; for some, this means statues of fairies, while others are simply surrounded by greenery.

Many of the roads of Lily Dale are narrow, stone pathways, and some of the mediums and psychics posts signs advertising availability. The small lake has a rowboat beckoning from the bank.

In other areas of Lily Dale are small parks, statues, fountains and gazebos with benches for rest, prayer and meditation. Strolling the grounds, don't be surprised if you venture down a winding, well-manicured path through the woods and encounter a prayer or healing session, especially at the site of the famous inspiration stump.

There is always so much to absorb from this peaceful place. I could linger for hours.

My friend Elaine Thomas, who lives in an old house on a corner lot with a low, private, stockade fence and a yard overgrown with greenery, has welcomed me to her home for over thirty years. I have always considered her my spiritual adviser. Year after year, I have enjoyed visiting this beautiful woman, who always tells me she sees a healing symbol on my forehead. She has never explained what it looks like in detail, just that it appears in the area where, as they say, you have a third eye. The third eye is believed to be the mystical, insightful, invisible eye between your eyebrows in the middle area of your forehead. It is thought to be your spiritual insight, and the source of outgoing as well as incoming wisdom and knowledge. My friend has never failed to remind me of what she sees and has always coaxed me to do something about it.

At one of our visits, she excitedly invited me to an open seminar she was holding with a Qigong Master (pronounced CHI or CHEE gong), Master Robert Peng. She said she had always believed I was meant to be some type of healer and that Qigong was a perfect path for me to follow. She reassured me she would be there.

On the day of the seminar I arrived early and found my way to the library where the event was to be held. This single story, hundred year old structure is fitted with old benches and walls lined with antique photographs. The attendees were three times the number the organizers had originally expected. The seminar was quickly moved to a much larger venue, the outdoor amphitheater, also a beautiful hundred year old structure, white, open, and breezy, easily handling two hundred attendees.

After a brief welcome and presentation of the rules, Master Robert Peng stepped onto the stage. He was small in stature with black hair and black framed glasses. He wore a simple black sweat suit with white stripes down the sides. When he began speaking in low, calm tones of broken English and Chinese, I found it nearly impossible to hear him and moved myself closer to the stage. In high school, I had always preferred sitting either in the middle or in the back of the classroom to avoid being chosen to answer, but on this occasion I was so interested in all the information being shared that, aside from the fact that it was easier to hear, I just had to be in the front row.

I simply did not want to miss a single word.

Master Peng told us how he was raised in China by a monk; he never told us how or why he was raised by this monk, but he said that when he was a child he had done a hundred day fast drinking only water and eating two dates per day. The monk taught Qigong, forbidden by the Chinese emperor and illegal to practice in China. The Emperor forbade the practice because he did not want the people to have such power. As a result, Peng secretly learned and secretly practiced Qigong. With the assistance of Australia's Prime Minister, Peng was fortunate to escape to Australia. He eventually found his way to the United States and to New York City, where he continues his practice today. In recent years, the discipline of Qigong has been reinstated in China, and you can find a class attended by as many as thirteen hundred people.

During this seminar, Master Peng taught us meditation and how to gather and collect energy—stamina energy and healing energy. I was hooked and amazed by the happiness I felt just being there. Then something crazy happened, and I thought I was losing my mind or that my imagination was running away with me. Watching Robert Peng speak, I saw a green glow radiate from him, a soft, green radiating light like that of a glow stick. I wish I could say I was joking, or making this up. I repeatedly turned away to see if it would go away, but whenever I turned back to watch Master Peng the green glow was still there. Later, against my better judgment, because I thought Elaine might convince me I had lost my mind, I shared my vision with her. Because she saw my excitement—and shared it—that I could see this glow, she insisted I tell Master Peng. I told him and, in a letdown, he made nothing of it, simply replying, "Oh, so you saw that?" Had he expected me to see the glow? At that moment, Qigong became a serious interest. I studied it for three years. Although I have many memorable stories from my Qigong experiences, two of them are most significant to this book.

The first occurred shortly after I had finished my Qigong studies. I received a call from another old friend, Debbie. She called because a mutual friend of ours had suffered a severe stroke and was in a coma. Her prognosis was not good: death seemed imminent. Debbie said the friend's husband knew I had studied under Robert Peng and asked if I would be willing to come to the hospital for a Qigong session on his wife. I later learned that he had also studied some sessions under Master Peng. The husband had run out of ideas and hope. I agreed to do this for them.

I told both Debbie and our friend's husband to meet me in the lobby of the hospital at six o'clock that evening. Hours prior to the meeting, I contacted Master Peng, told him the situation, and asked his advice about the technique I use. He was deeply receptive and gave sound advice.

When we met, I advised them both to think of this as a prayer session. The three of us entered the Intensive Care Unit, and I was reassured by the fact that the neurosurgeon and head ICU nurse would also be present. I felt quite comfortable knowing this, as their attendance was somehow calming.

We gathered around our friend's hospital bed and began with prayers. She lay so still. She looked as though she were already gone. The air in the room exuded despair, sadness, and hopelessness. I proceeded with a Qigong technique involving the balls of her feet (this area is referred to as the bubbling well). I used another technique involving her forehead (her third eye). God bless our friend, she awoke from the coma, eyes opening wide in apparent panic. Although still drug- induced, she was alert. She was unable to speak due to a ventilator, but her husband and Debbie talked to her. The doctor and nurse stayed quiet but supportive. The alertness lasted only a few moments before she drifted back to sleep, passing away later that night. But, to my surprise, her husband had nothing but gratitude toward me.

He was able to say goodbye to his wife—and he felt I had given that to him.

The second Qigong story most significant to me is even more personal, involving my own near departure from this world and the role Qigong played in my sticking around.

Nearly ten years ago, I was diagnosed with a bad gall bladder and was told it had to be removed. Now, I must step back a couple of years to explain that I have been a heart patient for a number of years and have had a few stents implanted, resulting in the need for blood thinners. The gall bladder surgeon at the local community hospital took me off these blood thinners until after the surgery, which seemed like a simple procedure—what could possibly go wrong?

How about everything?

I remember awaking in the recovery room and feeling pretty good, at least as good as anyone can feel immediately after surgery. I was rolled to my hospital room and greeted there by my wife Sally and a few friends. Everything seemed to be going well for maybe ten minutes, and then I began to feel minor pains in my chest and in my left arm. I shared this information with my wife, who wanted to summon a nurse. I asked her to wait while I evaluated the pain for myself, but seconds later, all hell broke loose! "Yep, go get the nurse," I yelled, but she was already halfway there.

After the nurse popped a couple of nitroglycerin pills under my tongue, I was rushed to the ICU and, shortly thereafter, transported to the Cardiac Care Unit of a local city hospital. This trip was supposed to have been by helicopter, but severe, snowy weather precluded a whirlybird ride; thus, I copped a bumpy trip in a simple—and claustrophobic—ambulance. My attendees were two stocky and wonderfully unflappable young ladies. The treacherous streets assured a challenging ride, and my overriding concern was for Sally, who was following us and alone.

Both vehicles arrived safely, however, and I remember sleeping, thankfully, quite peacefully. The next day, I awoke and had an angiogram, which revealed a large blood clot which had traveled to my heart after the gall bladder surgery. My treatment for the next two days was clot busters. I remained in the CCU. The day after the first angiogram, Wednesday, I developed pneumonia, which delayed a second angiogram and which made things even more interesting.

I steadily declined.

I became overwhelmed with anxiety watching my vital sign numbers go lower and lower. I was dying and couldn't do a damn thing about it. The only pain I really felt was watching the woman I love suffer watching the tragedy unfold—and then Sally said, "You're stronger than this; start fighting!" No one else in the world could ever get through to me like she could. I looked at her and told her to "Get me up and out of this bed!" I didn't care about how sore I was or how many tubes and wires were hanging off me, I had to get out of that bed. I was able to make it to the other chair in the room.

Sally called our friend Elaine Thomas in Lily Dale, the friend who had led me to the world of Qigong. Sally told her about my condition, and Elaine jumped into action. She called Robert Peng and advised me that the next day at 10 P.M., she and Master Peng and a large group of Qigong practitioners from across the country would conduct a remote healing on me. Sally left the hospital at 9:30 P.M. and by 10 I began practicing one of my favorite meditations and relaxing by listening to Jen Chapin music on my iPod.

I continued to do my best to pray.

At 10:30, I was done and ready to sleep, but I couldn't; for the longest time I lay in the bed awake, watching the clock turn eleven, twelve, one in the morning, two, three—I was getting frustrated and a bit angry as each hour passed. I wanted to sleep! Not until around 5 that morning did it occur to me: of course I can't sleep, I have been remotely loaded with Qi! The craziest part was that two hours later, the cardiologist entered the room and announced that all vital signs were normal, and I was going to be moved to a regular room. This was truly a miracle!

Before this event, I was unsure if I would ever leave that hospital.

The adventure was far from over. A second attempt to remove the clot failed, and I was then scheduled for bypass surgery. By now, however, the fear was gone, and Sally and I knew everything was going to work out fine.

I was spared and am here for a reason.

My adventure is a classic example of how East meets West in the world of medicine. Strangely though, I have never felt comfortable sharing Qi energy with humans. I rather use Qi energy with dogs.

Language is how we humans communicate. Have you ever noticed how much trouble we can get into using language? Dogs and other animals, however, seem not to have that problem; they communicate through energy. What they say, they mean, and what they mean, they say—no mistakes and no misunderstanding.

I have been using the communication of energy on animals for quite a while, in some ways to firmly influence them a little. Have you ever had someone approach you by coming too close and violating your personal space? You know how uncomfortable that is? Well, when I give a sit command, for example, and push the palm of my hand toward a dog, regardless of the distance—one foot, two feet, or eight feet—I hold my hand there and don't pull it away. Dogs are a hundred times more sensitive than we humans, and just holding my hand toward their faces and pushing my energy toward them and not removing my hand, they feel that space violation. They don't care for that sensation. This method has often stopped a dog from charging me. This action, in addition to my alpha disposition, prevents any fear or weakness. That is me, intimidating and gaining an alpha position. Using energy to enhance one's life and for a tool is really not as hocus-pocus as you may think. When you study Qigong and practice using energy, it all becomes quite logical and also simple.

The art of Qigong is learning how to gather and collect energy. This makes you a more powerful person. Before I visit a home that I know has a profoundly powerful breed that bites and/or is the problematic alpha character, I do my Qigong exercises to strengthen my own alpha power source so that when I enter the home, the pet immediately reads my power level. It's my belief that this aura I present keeps me safe. There is no detectable sense of weakness, and the dog respects that.

If you have the desire to investigate or to learn more about Qigong, I recommend you research it on the Internet. There are many sites available. Be mindful though, just because you research the discipline of Qigong, this doesn't mean you need to commit to it and follow only those precepts. You may just find some helpful hints. The significant point is to understand the power of energy and how it affects your dog. You may find that it piques your curiosity, and you may be interested to follow the way of Qigong yourself, maybe not for the ways I use it but for your own sense of well-being and confidence.

Let me share a quick story about communicating through energy and scent.

On a trip to California, I stayed with a family who had created a most beautiful back yard and outdoor kitchen, including a stone enclosed grill/bar combination. They were quite proud of their achievement but couldn't enjoy it due to their neighbor's two dogs. Any time the family tried to entertain, they were harassed by constant barking. These two dogs were so relentless, the family and guests were driven back into the house to party in peace.

The day I was there was Easter Sunday, and the family had planned a good sized party, and something needed to be done about the barking. So, about an hour before guests arrived, I placed a chair up against the solid wood fence, a finger in my ear to spare my hearing from the bark fest. These neighbor dogs had a fit over my closeness. Although they couldn't see me or get to me, they had my scent and my calmness. It took about fifteen minutes for them to start settling down, but they finally did. The message I had conveyed was, "I mean you no harm, and you have no need to threaten me." I did need to do this once more after the party started, but this time took only about five minutes to calm them down, and then they remained good for the rest of the afternoon.

One problem I did pick up was that, at times, my family's dogs were the instigators. So I found that when our dogs were corrected, the neighbor's dogs were more than happy to play along—again, communication without the use of words. Scent, calm energy, and patience had brought results.

I would hate to end this without mentioning a word about my good buddy Oliver. Oliver is a large black Standard Poodle, handsome as they come, and when we met he was a teenager who was about as wild as they get. His owner, Susan, a delightful senior, asked for some guidance on controlling Mr. Oliver. The training did not need to be too thorough because Oliver accepted direction and, therefore, learned quickly.

In reading Oliver, I found him quite interesting. His eyes were dark and deeply sad. My approach was utterly quiet. His home is large and beautiful, but to Oliver it didn't feel safe. The ceilings were sky high and the rooms seemed vast, almost cavernous in size. Everything was in its perfect place, including Oliver's beds—just perfect. Well, maybe perfect for a human, but to Oliver it was an immense space lacking security, a situation similar to a human feeling mild agoraphobia. When I arrived, Oliver gravitated to me immediately. I conveyed the message of peace to him, calm peacefulness.

On the flip side of this session, when I headed outside with Oliver to evaluate his outdoor behavior, he executed a complete one hundred and eighty degree change, a Dr. Jekyll and Mr. Hyde, if you will. He went completely out of control. Here, on this lakeside, fenced in, lush, and large backyard was even more space. Oliver must have covered every inch of this huge yard several times, missing not one blade of grass in his path. He ran like a freed prisoner. But, again, too much freedom is not what made Oliver happy; he felt like a ship without a rudder, flailing aimlessly. "Give me control, give me boundaries," he was screaming. Continuing to run, Oliver sideswiped me several times, appearing at times to be trying deliberately to knock me over. Increasingly evident he was simply not handling the outdoor space, I gave him a snap back into reality. When he approached me again in yet another attempt to knock me off my feet, I reached out and grabbed his collar. This maneuver nearly pulled my arm from its socket, but it also shocked Oliver and stopped him mid-stride. The look of shock on his face was almost comical, and worth the almost, shoulder dislocation.

That one instant of shock forever changed our relationship. A look of complete serenity filled his eyes and a calm thank you came over his expression that translated into, "I feel safe." Even now, when I see Susan, Oliver's owner, she jokes with me, saying, "When you walk into the room, Oliver sits and salutes!"

What I did with Oliver was simple: I read him. I understood him and made him feel safe, maybe for the first time ever. Freedom and space are fine for a dog for exercise, but they are not what our pets need for discipline and for overall well-being.

Direction and security bring our canine friends happiness.

I also noticed that Susan constantly talked and repeated commands. This constant verbalizing just confused Oliver. I finally told her, "You are doing a great job, but you talk too much." I suggested she stop talking to Oliver for the next forty-eight hours, never to stop communicating, but to stop talking. I wanted her to try to communicate only with energy. She could use the word no but nothing else. Acceptable were vocal noises: grunts, firm looks, hand motions, signals and pointing, but no words. I didn't wait forty-eight hours. I returned the next day to a deservedly proud woman. She now had Oliver's attention like never before. How gratifying to have Susan give Oliver a look, point a finger, and have him respond. I use this example almost every time I teach.

4
INQUIRING MINDS

When people learn what I do, they immediately ask a plethora of questions, such as, "What does it mean when my dog does this?" and, "What is that noise he makes; what is that weird behavior?" or, "Why does my dog...?" I love those questions, and answering with "I don't know" won't cut it.

The simple truth and the simple answer are that a dog's strange new habit or behavior is almost anxiety-based. "Why does my dog chase his tail?" and, "Why does he move his dog bowl around the room?" and, "Why won't he eat while another dog is in the vicinity?" or, "Why does he sit by me, and then whine?"

Anxiety!

What should you do about the anxiety driven behavior? Correct it. Your pet is not enjoying this behavior and state of mind. In fact, I call this the chasing his tail syndrome. When I see a dog chasing his tail, I correct him. What does he do? He stops, and looks up at me as if to say "thanks, I needed that." If you correct him by distracting him, you will change his current state of mind, no different from a human being stuck in a particular line of thinking: I can't stop worrying about finances; I can't sleep because I can't stop thinking about the paper or project due. You can't turn off your brain, but you certainly can distract your own thinking with, say, a movie or a run.

Here's what works for a dog. When his brain gets stuck, free him with a distraction. A simple example: when a dog sees another dog, his hackles stand up, and ears go up and forward. He becomes more and more excitable as the situation escalates. If I gently lay his ears back with the palms of my hands and tell him to relax, or I say, "Put your ears back," I can change his brain. I can calm him down.

A few years ago, a family found themselves in a sad situation: they had to surrender their Louisiana Catahoula Leopard dog. They were devastated but had no choice.

When I first met this dog, I was surprised by my own reaction. I thought, "Man, this may be the cutest dog I have ever laid eyes on!" He looked and acted more like a cartoon character than a dog. His coloring was merle—blue, white, brown, black and gray—a blend like a painting by an abstract artist. He weighed no more than twenty pounds soaking wet. He came up to me and propped on my foot, leaning on my ankle, and gazing up at me with big brown, long-lashed eyes as if saying, "I'm scared; will you protect me?" Catahoula dogs are supposed to be herding dogs, but I found it difficult to believe this guy was ever meant to herd anything larger than a lamb.

Now, I live by a hard rule when it comes to the shelter: I never adopt, not that I don't want to; if I did, there would be twenty rescues at my house, hindering my personal mission. I want the ability to temporarily take home the special needs dogs, who are food-aggressive, dog-aggressive, or disintegrating in the shelter environment. Again, these arrangements are temporary. Either I fix the aggression and return the dog to the shelter, or I adopt out to friends or family those dogs unable to handle returning to the shelter.

One Saturday morning, my wife accompanied me to the shelter. I told her to stay away from kennel #4, not wanting her to be schmoozed by the little Catahoula. Well, they met, and it was all over. A trip to the village clerk office and a rabies shot later, and we had a new pet. You just couldn't help falling in love with this cuddle toy. Everyone who met him fell in love. But within days, it became undeniable: Gus (his new name) had more issues than Time Magazine! He was no puppy, but you would never have known it from his behavior. He needed to be housebroken. He chewed and mouthed (this is when a dog puts your hand in their mouth but doesn't take a true bite). He wasn't good at keeping his food down because he ate too fast and had a delicate digestive system. We had to deal with several bouts of diarrhea.

"But he was so cute!"

He was certainly my hand-selected, greatest challenge. Gus' only hope was a lot of direction. He was overwhelmed with anxieties and severely damaged. He had no self-control. With constant training, however, and with the help of my thankfully steady Weimaraner/Lab mix dog Carley, Gus stood a chance. Within days, I saw improvements in Gus. All he needed in order to be adopted was a nice family with strong alpha leadership skills.

During a wonderful Christmas visit from my daughter Melissa, her husband, Eric, and my grandchildren, Liv and Chance, they decided Gus was moving to Colorado! He joined this beautiful family that also included two cats, Emma and Eve. Gus did great—at least for a while.

My daughter always enjoyed taking Gus for trail walks or for hikes in the desert. Suddenly, during one of their regular walks, Gus became dog aggressive. Without warning, Gus felt the need to protect my daughter, and sometimes my grandchildren, against all other dogs and people. While on the leash, he would strain and lunge at anything or anyone entering their common space.

This was alarming behavior cause for serious concern.

Not long after the onset of this behavior, I was en route to Colorado to evaluate Gus' new manner. Soon after arriving, Gus and I hit the trails for a walk. The scenery was astonishingly beautiful, trails winding alongside the river, calming and tranquil. Instantly, I noticed something was missing: Gus' aggression. He was enjoying the surroundings, sniffing and scurrying along.

I returned home and suggested that my daughter walk with us. The aggressive behavior reappeared. Like some rabid dog, Gus started pulling on the leash, rearing up on his hind legs and barking and straining aggressively at anything coming near. This surprised me because my daughter was no wallflower, no pushover; why was Gus acting like a protector? Then I realized Gus had sensed my daughter's anticipation of the acting out, and so had he.

You can't lie to a dog.

If you exhibit nervous or anxious energy, your dog feels that energy and reacts to it. Dogs know when you're happy or sad, tense or fearful—and they react to these emotions. You simply can't fool a dog because, remember, they communicate through energy.

After explaining this concept to my daughter, she focused on calmness and on energy. She realized that when she calmed, Gus calmed. There were still moments, however, when Gus became so excitable, he had to be placed on the ground on his side and allowed his hissy fit until he calmed down and relaxed. Sometimes this technique was repeated two or three times until he had worn out, expelled his bad energy, and relaxed.

Gus still lives happily with his loving family, but this is because they are a strong and spirited group. They understood the principles of energy and employed them with Gus. That's not to say that Gus, the Issue King, never finds new ways to annoy his family, but with the lessons I showed them and explained here, they will get through it.

An interesting discovery about dogs: they attempt to dispel their anxiety in many ways. One way is to run around and play, but there are other coping methods they use as well.

For example, if it is a forty degree day, but your dog is panting as though it's ninety degrees, he's not overheated, he's trying to deal with anxiety. It's yet another technique a dog will use to relieve his stress is yawning. I see this during training sessions. The dog is not tired, merely trying to deal. But what seems to be the most misunderstood behavior, and what I see primarily in smaller dogs such as a little Catahoula, is shaking. But don't be too concerned when Rover starts to rattle. I'm sure you've heard the expression "Shake it off"? Well, that's exactly what your dog is doing. He's okay; he's just trying to unwind.

Other questions I've been asked include: "Why does my middle age dog chew the rug?" and, "Why does my Husky all of the sudden dig holes in the yard?" or, "Why does she chase her tail and push her dog dish around the kitchen floor after I just filled it?" Again, these are types of anxious behaviors that you can help your dog correct with your calm and definite energy. If humans could do the same, mental health doctors would go out of business.

One more example (just in case I haven't yet driven home my point.) I recently met a dog named Spencer, an eighty pound, handsome black and white Australian Shepherd/Border Collie mix. His family told me he drives them a bit crazy by lying around and whining. He stops only when you pet him. What do we do? Correct him. A snap of the fingers along with a scolding "No," and Spencer stops whining. If you pet him, however, you're only encouraging the whining—the unwanted behavior.

A good example of how an anxiety manifests itself into something worse: Spencer became so anxious, he actually stopped eating. For two days, we tried to solve this mystery. Was it the dish soap? Was something wrong with the food? Was Spencer under the weather? And then, while observing the overall picture, an unexpected little answer appeared—maybe not that little. We determined the problem was the forty pound English bulldog Pippa, Spencer's two-year-old roommate. We noticed that Pippa, always fed separately from Spencer, thus claiming Spencer's dish. Big, tough Spencer didn't know what to do. To remedy the situation, we first removed Pippa from the room so Spencer had no distractions, and then we took pieces of food from the bowl and hand fed Spencer. He accepted this ritual. Eventually, I held the bowl, and Spencer began feeling comfortable enough again to eat from his bowl. Subsequently, Spencer reclaimed his bowl, and Pippa was no longer allowed to use Spencer's bowl, nor was she allowed to be in the room while Spencer ate. This eating problem had nothing to do with the whining behavior, but any unwelcome behavior is a problem stemming from an anxiety—that you can correct.

Let's talk further about some of the common complaints I hear, "Fido loves to take and sometimes eat my socks." Socks hold a boatload of your scent.

That is why they are so attractive to our pets. What do we do about it?

There is a ritual I do with dogs to teach them the difference between objects they may or may not have. Sit in the floor with your pet and with six items: two items he may have, such as a chew toy and a ball; and four items he may not have, such as a sock, cell phone, a remote control, or a child's glove. Encourage him by praising him if he chooses the toy or ball, and give him a firm "No" correction if he goes for the other items. Remember, issue a quiet, but firm, "No," because issuing a loud "No!" only raises the excitement, the opposite of the desired result.

I was once told, "My Husky loves to dig holes in the yard". Huskies are famous for digging holes in the yard, because they like to stay cool by digging a hole and lying in it. "Ahhh, that feels good!" But you correct it. Find them a nice cool place; or find them a shaded cement floor to lie on.

Now it's time for coprophagia: the desire to eat poop. This behavior unsettles just about any dog owner. Although some believe there may be some deficiency in the dog's diet causing this behavior, you can correct it. I suggest you show the dog the feces and give him a firm correction while offering him an extremely tempting replacement, something with an overwhelming, positive aroma. Taste buds are not a dog's strongest sense—but smell is. His lack of taste buds is why he is able to eat poop in the first place, and so take advantage of his eighty-eight million plus smell receptors, by offering something such as cooked chicken, and you'll win the battle. Some other theories are that if a dog eats too much too fast, the food doesn't have time to digest, still smelling like dog food when he evacuates his system. Slow down his eating habit either by hand feeding or by using a spiral food bowl. Finally, adding pineapple to the dog's food can help add an undesirable scent to the excrement, further deterring the behavior as well.

"A problem I am having with my dog," a wonderful client of mine once told me, "is that he bolts out of the door and out of sight, returning only when he feels like it." This is a uniquely touchy subject I will address carefully because a lot of people disagree with me. Please believe me, I am only trying to save your pet's life. A dog rarely survives being struck by an automobile. Start by teaching the pet about the invisible line: just because a door is open doesn't mean he is allowed to pass through it. This is accomplished with red leash training. If saving your pet's life requires more desperate and serious measures, I believe you need to install an underground fence system or resort to an

E-Collar. If possible, find a qualified dog trainer, one agreeing with this method. Have the trainer assist with the E-collar process. A good E-collar has a noise setting on it, and that may be enough to be effective. If not, I suggest you use the shock method. There are different settings, and your dog responds to a light shock. A qualified dog trainer can help you with the amount of shock.

The reason I prefer you get help from a professional about using either method is that I fear over-shocking; while these shocks are effective, they may also may be a bit traumatic for you dog. I have seen sensitive dogs suffer from bouts of diarrhea after this training. Some even attempt to run away, the wrong way, from the sensation. Keep the shock as low as possible, and encourage your pet to come to you. He needs to think that returning to you will solve his problem. The collar controller or transmitter should be in the trainer's hand, not yours. In essence, you need to be the savior.

I am often asked, "Does my dog need company?" and, "Should I adopt a second dog?" Company is a nice concept, but who will the second dog belong to: to you or to the first dog? It's a good question to consider. Truth is, you are his company. You are all the pack he needs. You are the powerful alpha. This has always been my brand of dog math: one dog is one dog's worth of work. Two dogs are four dogs' worth of work; three or more dogs can just get crazy. I am absolutely not trying to discourage anyone from adopting a second dog; simply be sure it is something you're doing for yourself and not for your first dog.

Additionally, I'm likely to strongly discourage you from ever adopting litter-mates. Puppies are cute, and it may seem like a sweet move to have brother and sister grow up together, but it's a recipe for disaster. These two cute creatures will never—and I mean never—need you. They have one another. Thus, as far as they are concerned, you are secondary and a tagalong. I have seen this scenario several times, and it has almost always developed into a bad situation. You are not the true alpha; you are more like a servant. For best results in raising a puppy, the puppy needs to need you.

Ultimately, the three most serious questions clients ask are about dog aggression, separation anxiety, and food aggression.

Dog aggression, discussed earlier when we introduced Gus, the Louisiana Catahoula dog, is a fear issue, and this fear can be cured by socialization and by correction. Walking your dog with confidence in the heel position through dog-populated areas means your pet has no choices and must follow your lead. Heeling your dog in a forward motion in conjunction with the confidence you exude guides your dog through this gauntlet. If this technique doesn't work or is just not enough, roll your dog on his side, hold him down, and help him through the hissy fit until he wears out and calms down—and trust me, they will.

If, while walking your dog-aggressive pet, your dog gets involved in a fight, do not grab the dogs by the collars. You will surely be bitten. I recommend breaking up the fight by grabbing tails. Be careful, because you can still get bitten, but rest assured you will break up the fight. Another point I want to to make is that, when I am approached by other aggressive dogs, I keep my dog in the heel position and confront the oncoming dog with an outstretched hand, a loud "Hey!" and with a slight forward motion, thereby positioning myself as the alpha and pushing my energy and attitude toward them. This has always seemed to work for me.

One year, I was asked: "What can be done about separation anxiety?" This is also an issue of fear, but less correction is involved. We humans tend to telegraph to our dog all types of information building up to our departure. They watch us grab our coats and keys and go through several rituals leading up to our walking out the door. This raises the dog's energy but also his anxiety. We would not leave our car and walk away with the motor still running, which is what we are doing to our pet when leaving in a high state of emotion. When possible, we need to change our behaviors, to coax the dog into a calm state and to slip out the door with little indication. The point is, if we leave our dog in a calm state, he will remain in a calm state. A kennel can also help in this situation. Most importantly, leave your house with your dog in a calm state.

Another serious concern of my clients has been food aggression. I will mention a technique that I use, but you will read much more about it in the story about Bear the Rottweiler. Food aggression is indeed a fear—a fear of starvation. It's also a drive for survival. The technique I use is to claim the dog food, letting Fido know that it is mine, and that I am willing to share it with him.

Step one? Run your hands through his dog food, permeating it with your scent. I prefer dry dog food because the second step is to hand feed only one piece at a time until you become confident the dog is relaxed—and dry dog food makes that a bit easier.

Step three, eventually let your dog eat out of the bowl while you hold the bowl approximately a foot or so above the floor. Again, when you feel confident, place down the bowl with a small amount of food in it—maybe just enough to cover the bottom of the bowl. Repeat this process approximately four or five times until he gets the usual amount of dinner. I also suggest you do this for several days until feeding time becomes a calm experience. When you are in a multiple dog situation, you will always have to be cautious. As stated earlier, you will probably need to feed the dogs separately, but this assures safety for the humans.

One more thing I want to say regarding the question I am also often posed: "Why is my dog afraid of thunderstorms?" Aren't we all afraid of things we don't understand? Although we don't know the cause of phobias, we do know they exist, and dogs, too, need to feel secure. Have you ever seen the dog coats that are placed on your dog to help them cope with thunderstorms? Well, the reason these coats enjoy a degree of success is because they represent the mother dog's mouth gently squeezing the shoulders of her pups, making them feel secure by calming them. If your dog gets nervous or anxious, try this technique by gently squeezing your dog's shoulders with your hands. This gesture makes your dog feel secure. You will feel your dog relax.

5
SPANKY
THE GHOST
HUNTER

You know the saying, "If you're lucky enough to live on a lake, you're lucky enough?" On one of those perfect autumn evenings with cool temperatures, the scent of fallen leaves was pervasive and a full orange moon reflected off the water. But for hundreds of squawking Canada geese, the lake was placid. The setting could not have been more appropriate for the phone call I received while reposing in this serene setting, a call prompted partly by the fact that Halloween crept around the corner.

A gentleman on the other end of the line said, "I don't want you to think I'm crazy or that this is a prank call, but..."

He thought maybe his twelve year old American pit bull Spanky may have seen a ghost in his house. He wanted my opinion on the situation and wondered if I thought a ghost in the house was a real possibility. I opined that while dogs are highly sensitive to energy, I was unsure whether I believed in ghosts! I wanted to go with the ghost theory, however. Spanky was so afraid to be inside the house, he was staying next door at the man's mother's house. I agreed to meet with the family the following morning in order to investigate the unusual behavior and to assess the situation. I hung up the phone wondering what I had gotten myself into this time.

The next morning brought a crystal clear blue sky and a brisk breeze. I left early for the appointment because I wanted to appraise the neighborhood. The village was a petite, quaint farming enclave. I spotted a small Mom & Pop convenience store and a feed store but little else; I didn't even see a gas station.

I located the mother's house first, a pretty, white prefabricated house with a well-groomed yard, and the house next door, which I assumed to be the home of the client and of Spanky, a two-story, century old house in need of paint, not just a fresh coat; the house had no paint at all. All the windows were intact, but the clapboards were loose, and some of the eaves drooped slightly.

I'm not one to judge a person's house, because in 1985 I was in a similar situation, perhaps an even worse one. After my divorce, I was a ship without a rudder and needed a home. A good friend told me to get into the car. We rode for a seeming eternity. We drove away from city buildings and businesses to houses farther and farther apart until we found ourselves in the country. We stopped in front of a dilapidated house. Dilapidated is the best word to describe it. "You see this house?" said my friend, "Well, it's broken just like you. You both need one another, so buy it and heal together."

I did.

I purchased it for fifteen thousand dollars, probably about fourteen thousand, nine hundred dollars too much. The Greek Revival structure had been built in 1823. What really sold me on it despite the seeming neglect was the perfectly straight roofline with no hint of sagging. Much like me, this house had hope.

Once I roamed through the house, I counted thirty-two broken windows and a couple dozen chickens living in the likely dining room with armies of rats and cockroaches. A tame bunny rabbit scampered freely, belonging now to no one. Above all, though, the greatest aspect of healing about this house was the knowledge my current wife lived in the village, an added blessing.

Thus, I saw the metaphorical parallel of the unpainted, love-starved house to my situation. I pulled into the driveway of the mother's house and immediately heard an elderly bark behind the front door. I strode to the house and knocked on the front door. The owner, a seventy year old woman with white hair and a sweet, cheerful disposition, opened the door. At her feet was an old American Pit Bull named Spanky. It was obvious Spanky had suffered at least one damaging stroke: the left side of his face and his left eye drooped. His nails were grossly long, and his white and black coat looked worn out, a little like his expression. Although this oldtimer appeared pathetic, he was in no way impeded by advanced age, or intimidated by anything.

I fell for him immediately.

The first order of business was to go for a walk with Spanky. This is how I establish myself as the alpha character and let Spanky know I can be trusted. I could find nothing unusual about Spanky or his behavior, and so I decided to check out this suspicious "Twilight Zone" of a house.

Spanky, his owner, and I entered through the front door. The visibly old house fit the cliche for a haunted one, and, although I wouldn't have been too terribly shocked to have been greeted by Herman Munster, I was still skeptical about the ghost story.

We paused momentarily to sit on the enclosed front porch for time to evaluate Spanky before we proceeded. He seemed okay, but it was clear to me that he preferred to have been outside. One detail arousing my suspicion on the porch was a large ashtray brimming with cigarette butts. Maybe it didn't bother Spanky, but its pungent, acrid odor unnerved me. Spanky did seem mildly nervous and a bit sketchy, but it was upon entering the living room that Spanky became unglued. He wanted out. He kept trying to head back toward the front door. I'm about six feet four inches tall and weigh about two hundred and fifty pounds, but I had a hard time containing this muscular animal. I hadn't sensed fear, only clear anxiety, a focus on getting out of there.

The interior of the home was clean and neat and warmly homey. The first thing I noticed in the living room was a cage with a pair of large Amazon Macaw parrots, and I wondered whether they were scaring Spanky. I led him over to the birds and got no significant reaction other than his hankering to head for the front door. And then I remembered Spanky had extremely long nails and the kitchen's linoleum floor: maybe the nails on linoleum created a slippery floor and caused his distress—so far, no ghosts; but plenty of possibilities for his agitation.

The next thing I noticed was an antiquated wood-burning stove in the living room and an empty bag from wood pellets in the kitchen trash. I asked the owner how he heated his home, whether with wood only or by augmenting with a furnace. He said he used natural gas, mostly. I asked how old the furnace was. "Very old," he said. I had noticed that he and another resident had shared a bad cough, and he explained its origin: cigarettes. I asked how long they'd been coughing; when he replied, "Only a few days," I asked: "Is that when Spanky sees his ghost?" The answer was, "Yes."

I suggested they quickly get the house checked for carbon monoxide. Sure enough, that turned out to have been the problem. There were four people living in this house; it became my belief and the belief of Spanky's owner, that Spanky is nothing short of a hero and that they owe their lives to 'Spanky the ghost hunting dog.'

Moral of the story: listen to your dog. This story was fun and managed to make some newspapers. Listen to your dog. Dogs are a thousand times more sensitive than humans in the scent department. Pay attention to their moods, body language, and, most of all, to their behavior. Spanky's behavior conveyed a message, a warning, and ignoring it could have proven deadly. Communication is a two way street; happily, they did their best to listen, and Spanky did his best to tell them what he needed.

A note: just because a dog is watching out for his family, don't automatically assume that he is demanding the alpha position. He is likely just one of those wonderful animals who cares for, loves, and watches out for his family.

6
"SHE'S MINE, I TELL YOU"

My son Jake is a professional actor in a nearby city. I have watched his performances since he played Thomas Edison in a one man show in sixth grade. He spent the entire show dressed in white, sitting astride an eight-foot ladder surrounded by clouds and narrating from heaven the life of Edison. I remember thinking how remarkable that this child remembered all of his lines, hundreds of them, and conveyed so many emotions and thoughts.

Many times since have I watched Jake replay this type of scenario, from high school through his professional career. He is now thirty-six and an incredible actor. There have been many occasions when, watching him on stage, I wondered where he got such a gift. My wife believes he inherited it from me. At first I was skeptical, but then I thought of how I've used acting in my professional life, and I realized she might be onto something.

As a municipal and Railroad Police officer, I have through the years experienced many moments requiring a need to act, whether to catch a bad guy or to persuade a dog that I am the alpha, either to establish dominance or simply to reclaim something the dog has claimed for its own. In any case, I have used my acting ability as a resource, and the tale I tell you is a strong example example.

This railroad cop has worked some of the darkest, scariest, rat- infested places on earth. One railroad in Buffalo is called Tower T. (Railroad locations and yards are primarily named after letters such as T, IQ, or QX due to the old telegraph system.) Tower T had become a problem area because many trains stopped in that area, leaving them vulnerable. Much of what you own travels by train: automobiles, furniture, clothes, electronics, and food. Thus, when a merchandise-laden train stops, it attracts thieves. This is why railroad cops originated. They are independently commissioned. Each city has a Commissioner with the licenses for each department, and every officer works under this license. Many times I traveled across state lines and barged into a village police station, my unfamiliar face garnering strange, suspicious glances until I explained my commission.

Back at Tower T, we realized we must target this area for protection and set up surveillance. We were a team of two: one officer's beat was area streets, and the other hid himself in the bushes near the most recent train break-ins. I was the guy set up in the brush. Fortunately for me, a particular incident occurred during warm weather, assuring no noisy shivering in the cold. What we did contend with, however, was intense darkness. Our location was high above the street lights, at times so dark, we literally could not see our hands in front of our faces—quite a challenge to see details. Also, there were rats. You couldn't see them, but you could hear them scuttling around your feet, and at times they sang, an unmelodic but eerie, unsettling series of noises. Whatever the weather, and no matter how many rats serenaded you, you had to focus on your mission to protect the valuables on your train by catching the thieves. Just like walking a dog for the first time or working with a family to better their dog's behavior, distractions must be quashed, and the mission at the moment must be kept at the forefront of your mind.

On one such night, while hiding in the overgrowth, a container train coasted into view. I waited. At around three o'clock A.M., I heard the clanging of trailer doors opening. I was excited; it was happening. I could hardly see a thing in the dense darkness, but I could make out shadowy figures clambering aboard the trains. I was unable to count how many there were and therefore focused on one and moved forward.

I sneaked up on this person and reached out to grab his ankles to yank him from the train, but the train suddenly jerked and inched forward. The guy jumped off the train on the opposite side from where I had lunged for him. He had never seen me; it was just dumb luck he had jumped off on the other side. I waited until the train cleared, a seeming eternity. Just when it was time to search again for the guy, another train rolled in, delaying any possible attempt to nab the suspect. Ten more minutes elapsed before both trains were out of my way, but I wondered if there was any chance the gang would remain in the area. Here I employed another technique I'll talk about later: follow through. I knew my chances of catching up with the guy were slim, but there was a chance. I kept my eyes and mind open, and I was rewarded.

About eighty yards up the tracks, I spotted the barely visible glow of a cigarette, presenting another dilemma: if I approached, they would hear the brush under my feet and would scatter like rats. I summoned my acting ability. Rather than trying to sneak up on them without their hearing me, I decided to run down the tracks in their direction screaming in a high pitched, girlish voice: "Help me! Help me! They're trying to kill me!" The startled gang froze in their tracks, in wonderment at this screeching person running down the tracks. Apparently, I was convincing enough that they remained paralyzed in shock, allowing me to rush them, pull out my weapon, and scream in my natural voice, "F**k you!" They screamed in alarm, still unaware of who I was because of my plain clothes; they seemed relieved when I finally yelled, "Freeze! Police!" All four of them actually seemed happy I was a policeman rather than a homicidal maniac and, of one accord, assumed the prone position before hearing the command! When the backup police car pulled up a hundred yards away, separated from us by a field and a chain link fence, they readily obeyed my orders to march to the car, climbing over that fence and admitting themselves into the back seat of the police cruiser!

I shared this acting story to illustrate that, although it's impossible to hide your emotions from a person or dog, you can be theatrical enough to make your point. You can convince the dog that you mean what you say, getting your desired results.

I have used this tactic many times. One of my favorite examples is a request to visit a couple in their sixties. They had no children still at home, but they had a three-year-old female German Shepherd named Lottie. Lottie was gorgeous with all the classic markings of a German Shepherd. The couple reported that Lottie was biting and had even bitten them. They needed help. Could anything be done? They loved her and wanted to do what they could, but a German Shepherd biting her owners is a particularly serious matter. I had never before requested a dog be muzzled before my arrival, but in this case it seemed prudent.

I arrived at the home my customary way: knocking, entering, and letting the pet greet me. I always like to see what the dog will do on its own. In this case, however, instead of meeting me, Lottie was too busy attempting to remove her muzzle. This wasn't working as planned. I had one of the owners remove the muzzle and hoped for the best. To everyone's relief, Lottie was fine. She politely sniffed me and walked away. Nothing to do here.

After a few minutes conversing with the owner, I took Lottie for a walk, a standard ritual for me when I meet a dog: red leash, heeling control, etc.—it's like getting a patient's vital signs from a canine behavioral standpoint. All seemed to go well. As previously mentioned, in these first five to ten minutes I typically establish myself as the alpha character. I convey to the dog that I am the boss and don't care much about what the dog has to say, at least not yet. I will listen to the dog after I gain trust. I strived to gain Lottie's trust.

During the walk, Lottie managed to slip the leash. Naturally, I was rather embarrassed to walk quickly back to the owners and say, "Can you help me retrieve your dog?" This situation had never happened before. As for Lottie, life was great: the sun shone brightly, and the breeze was warm and redolent with millions of different scents. She ran from yard to yard as though this new found freedom would last forever, but her freedom ended abruptly when the owner helped me trap her in a neighbor's garage. I was relieved that she had been retrieved quickly, particularly apprehensive she would bite a neighbor, presenting a much more serious situation.

The most interesting aspect of Lottie's escape was that, after capture and a leash draped around her neck, her face expressed peace. She panted and smiled up and licked my hand as though saying, "That was fun, but it was scary." She seemed not at all regretful about being restored to the leash.

When we got back to the house, I noticed Lottie was all over the male owner, jumping and mounting. I realized Lottie claimed a lot of ownership: this was not a man owning a dog but a dog owning a man. I corrected Lottie with the red leash. She seemed to take it well and sat obediently at my side. But when the lady of the house arrived, things really got peculiar: Lottie jumped all over her. I corrected Lottie again with the red leash.

While the husband, wife, and I discussed the dog at the kitchen table, the lady reached down to pet Lottie on the head. Big mistake: Lottie attacked and lunged for the hand and arm that had petted her just seconds earlier. This was not so much aggression, however, as correction: Lottie was clearly giving the owner a correction. Alpha wolf was saying, "I touch you; you don't touch me."

The couple froze while the Shepherd dominated them. I took advantage of the scene and leaped at Lottie to show I was the boss. She backed down instantly. The owners and I enjoyed a long conversation about the environment that had been created in the household and how dangerous this situation was: without guidance, Lottie could become a red zone case and a great liability. This dominance would not improve on its own, and with time this problem would only get worse. Someone was going to get seriously injured and could result in Lottie becoming labelled a dangerous dog—or worse.

The wife and I took Lottie outside to practice heeling and control with the red leash. While on our walk, a peculiar incident occurred: Lottie growled and barked at me and lunged at the lady. Fortunately, I had control of the leash and gave Lottie correction. Unfortunately, that didn't stop Lottie's bad behavior. I had an idea to claim ownership of this lady from the German Shepherd. As silly as that sounds, what I did next might seem even sillier: I sat the growling dog and began stroking the lady's arm, all the while telling Lottie in a strong, firm voice, "Mine, she's mine." I continued to stroke the lady's arm and to proclaim, "Mine, mine!" to Lottie. The poor lady could only exclaim, "Good Lord, I hope the neighbors aren't watching!" We laughed.

This ritual continued for hardly a minute, until I could see by the look in Lottie's eyes that she had conceded, conveying, "Okay, she's yours." We continued our lesson with no problems at all, and the owner walked proudly. It was a gratifying moment.

This case was unique but easy to understand. The dog had detected weakness in the home and had assumed the role of alpha, not because she wanted to, but because she felt obligated to for the survival of the pack. The result was that Lottie was a very unhappy dog because of the pressure of assuming alpha status over her human pack, an unfair position for Lottie to have been placed in, her sadness clearly visible in her eyes and in her unbalanced behavior. The remedy for Lottie had been direction mixed with a healthy dose of good pack leader dominance. Correction had helped Lottie escape her confused state and had undoubtedly enabled her to smile again.

Lottie's situation is fairly common. When a dog knows who the leader, the alpha, is, he or she is happier and calmer. Understanding who's boss benefits everyone in the household.

7

THE YORKIE
WITH THE
FIFTY-FIVE
GALLON
BLADDER

Living in a rural area, I try to keep my appointments within a thirty mile radius. My visits tend to be two, sometimes three hours long. If the driving is reasonable, the day seems less taxing, and for a retired man, time is always at a premium. Not only am I concerned about leaving my own dogs home alone for too long, but the ages old retirement mantra is true: "When did I ever have enough time to work?" Somehow, the days are very full.

My latest trip was slightly longer than usual, but I made an exception after a request from a friend to help someone absolutely desperate. This friend of my friend had two Yorkshire Terriers who were ruining the house. This was all the information I was given, but I was game. I love a good challenge.

They lived about ninety minutes from my house, but it was a beautiful day for a ride: blue skies and warm fresh air, and I had all the time in the world for a change, and so off I went. Arriving at the house, I could see why, if her house was being ruined, the owner would be upset: it was a brand new, incredibly pristine house with a yard to match. In fact, the entire neighborhood was brand new. The house was easy to find, despite the many winding streets, because there were only about fifty homes. Much of the surrounding properties were still vacant lots, but the house and yard I was summoned to see were so complete that trees were growing, and the lawn lush and needing mowing, the property presenting a stark contrast to surrounding ones, like an oasis in a desert.

Approaching the large, double front doors, I could already hear barking inside. The yips and yaps continued until the door opened, at which time the barking immediately ceased, but I was tag teamed by two Yorkshire Terriers jumping all over my legs. After correcting the jumping, which they readily accepted, they started running up and down the long hallway toward the back of the house and jumping all over the living room furniture, as though they considered the entire house their personal jungle gym. The owner and I herded them into a section of the kitchen, where she corralled them into a corner in order to protect the rest of the house.

They were two of the cutest little guys you'd ever want to meet, and the majority of the behavior problems were easy fixes, but one problem was not at all minor: one of them had a problem going potty outside. No matter how long a walk or how long outside, he felt compelled to wait until he got back inside the house to relieve himself. I decided to see for myself. Like all other dog visits, we headed outside; I was determined we were going to stay outside until he did the necessary, if we had to wait until we heard cowbells jangling home.

The summer day offered much sound and scent to a little dog: dive-bombing birds, bugs underfoot, fluttering leaves in the breeze, trundling bicycles and passing cars and freshly mown grass permeating even human nostrils. Roars from the nearby municipal airport caught his attention, too. Fully seduced by his surroundings, he showed no fear, only interest.

After nearly an hour of walking and exploring these intriguing things, I felt a bit weary and out of ideas. At one point, I found a fire hydrant and tried to lift his rear leg, without result. By now, I would gladly have hiked my own leg up if it would have helped. Suddenly, I noticed that his eyes, ears, and nose had become extremely busy.

What was the problem? The problem was that he was too fascinated and too busy to pee. In his mind, he thought, "I can do that when I go back inside the boring old house!"

I noticed a construction site across the street. I said to myself, "No grass, no objects, and no trees."

Nothing but a plain, dried up mud patch with nothing to investigate.

We entered this plot of nothing and merely waited—and waited. We didn't move: there was absolutely nothing to sniff or to check out.

Then? Bang! The floodgates opened.

The little guy almost flooded the neighborhood. That was it! He was just too busy outside with all the wonderful things the world offered to be bothered with that potty business! I must admit, I thought I would be forced to concede on this one, but mud was the answer. I received a follow up call a few weeks later: we had a convert and no more messes in the house.

The second Yorkshire Terrier turned out to be a routine situation. She took direction very well and sincerely wanted to cooperate. She certainly made up for the challenges her brother had brought to the home.

Another observation I made recently is that, when I find myself in a challenge, such as outwitting my little Yorkie friend, I am reminded of one of my favorite follow through stories. I could have given up in frustration but realized that follow through is far more important than simple patience, especially when dealing with our canine friends. Follow through is the most important ingredient for success in nearly any situation. Indeed, it can sometimes be the difference between life and death. Follow through is more powerful than patience. Follow through until the end, until you get the desired result.

A personal experience where follow through could have proven to be a matter of life and death happened years ago. I was earning my pilot's license, and part of the process was completing a long distance, cross-country solo flight. My plan involved a flight from Buffalo, New York to Watertown, New York near the Adirondack Mountains. Just a rookie pilot, I appreciated the safety precaution of a flight plan and the knowledge that the air traffic controller kept an eye on me for the duration of the flight.

The Buffalo air traffic controller monitored me until Rochester took over, and from there I reached Syracuse air space and was passed over to the Burlington, Vermont controller, where the excitement began. My radio started breaking up. Seconds later, it died. This should have been no problem, because a safety feature of the airplane was two radios, the case on every plane. In fact, there are two of almost everything you might need in each plane: two sticks/steering wheels, two sets of pedals, magnets, altimeters, etc. When my radio went kaput, I simply switched to the backup radio, only to discover it was also dead. And then I noticed both fuel tank gauges read empty. The hair on the back of my neck rose in porcupine mode. Wait a minute, I said to myself, if I'm out of fuel, why am I still flying? I realized the fuel tank gauges were electrical, which meant I was actually experiencing total electrical failure. This moment became my first epiphany—follow through. Don't panic. Think. What does all this mean? Again, follow through.

The reason the airplane motor was still firing without electricity was the same reason your lawnmower runs without a battery—the magnetos. I had two, enabling the plane to continue flying, and I knew I had enough fuel, because I had remembered to fill her up before leaving Buffalo.

The Syracuse airport was now in sight. I decided to land there, although, without radio availability, I would have to fly in unannounced. With commercial jets coming in and out of Syracuse, it was going to be very dangerous. So, again, follow through: keep my act together, evaluate, and follow through to my destination.

I decided to head for the Watertown airport, if I could find it. I followed the Lake Ontario shoreline until spotting the St. Lawrence Seaway, and I followed it until seeing some of the Thousand Islands. Within twenty minutes, the rotating beacon of the Watertown airport beckoned. Using my newest revelation of follow through, I knew my flaps were electrical and therefore impossible to operate manually. The purpose of the flaps is to lose altitude at a faster rate and to slow down the airplane. This was very unnerving, but follow through was crucial. Wanting to land into the wind, I flew over the airport once to gauge wind direction; also, if the tower saw me arriving unannounced, the controller would realize I was in distress.

I had made it this far, and it was time for follow through with the landing and, in the spirit of follow through, I planned to kiss the ground. I made a long pattern to see any other traffic in the area, and with a very long final swoop, brought her in without flaps. When I touched down, I was moving so fast I nearly had to stand on the brakes. I used every inch of that runway. But I was down, and I was safe.

Every element of this emergency was about follow through. After I parked the airplane and climbed up the stairs of the tower, I got strange stares from everyone. I asked if there was a mechanic on duty, and everyone relaxed with a nod of understanding, conveying, "Oh, that explains everything."

I realize this analogy seems a bit strained, a long way from a Yorkshire Terrier with issues in the mud pit, but there is a very important correlation. The Yorkie required patience, and most dogs needing my help do, but the follow through gets you the best results. Be the alpha, lead—and follow through.

With these four-legged guys, you just never know the catalyst or the moment of truth. I preach the walk. The walk fixes almost everything, but standing still in boring mudville made the difference in this case. Who knew? I guess that's why I call my furry clients my little professors. They are always teaching me—if I am paying attention, that is.

8
THE INCIDENTAL EXPERIMENT

On a warm balmy Summer evening, I was sitting on my front deck with my wife when I received a distressed call from our local Animal Control officer, who had just received a call from the State Police. They reported that an unknown person complained to them about a resident living adjacent to the state land who had over fifty dogs. The State Police further told the Animal Control officer that their initial investigation revealed that allegedly all fifty dogs were said to be stuffed into three small travel kennels. How could this be? I could not wait to learn more about this situation.

The Animal Control officer continued, the location was a secluded plot of state hunting land. She, along with the State Police and local Sheriff's department, had arranged to meet at 7 A.M. the next morning to raid the property. She sounded a bit overwhelmed; she could not imagine such a situation, and had no real idea what to expect. She asked if I were available to assist with the raid and to help handle the dogs. I would never have missed this opportunity and readily agreed to meet them at the property.

I got to thinking about that area and realized how many years I had spent hunting up there. If anyone wanted to conduct clandestine activity, this was certainly the neighborhood for it due to a limited number of residences, most of whom were set back from the road and hidden by woods. Suddenly, I remembered I knew someone living close to the site, and I phoned him, asking if he was aware of these dogs or of any such inhumane activity in the area. He knew exactly what I was talking about and said that only two properties away from his were frequent outbursts of barking dogs—many dogs. He could tell by the pitch that these were not large dogs but were Chihuahua type dogs. On more than one occasion, the cacophonous concert of barking had inspired area coyotes to follow suit, disturbing all peace. When I asked how long he'd endured this situation, he said for about three weeks.

Arriving the following day, we could hardly believe our eyes: in three small carriers languished forty-four Chihuahua-size dogs, one deceased, all others terrified and caked in urine and feces. Lassoing them with red leashes required artfulness to avoid being bitten, but we rounded them all up and transported them to the animal shelter.

At the shelter, our first task was to triage them one at a time with a local veterinarian, who said all seemed likely to survive but that all of them had been diagnosed with a heart murmur. We assembly-lined them through several volunteer dog groomers, and they started to look more like dogs, but they certainly were not acting like dogs: not one of the forty-three was barking. We discovered that not one of the pups seemed familiar with grass; they seemed afraid of it, and they recoiled from human touch.

Local news stations visited the shelter and reported the story, and subsequently dozens of volunteers flocked to the shelter. For more than a week, shelter traffic became unprecedented. Some arrived from distant miles either to spend time with the dogs (holding them and helping them understand the human bond) or to adopt one; others generously donated food, towels, cleaning products or money. The outpouring of concern was unlike any other humanitarian enterprise I had ever seen in a small county, the response making me very proud to be a western New Yorker.

As for the incidental experiment, initially, we placed the dogs in pens in groups of three, four, or five. Immediately, a pecking order developed: one dog in each kennel seemed to claim alpha position/pack leader. That alpha was the pushy one and might even claim all the food, biting the others to show that he meant business.

Suddenly, I had an idea.

Each night, I mixed and matched the dogs in different groups within the pens and watched the results of the new pack creations. Within minutes, a new pecking order began: the alpha from yesterday may be the omega today, lowest on the totem pole, and vice versa. This was quite an education. We realized while shifting dogs among the kennels that each night the pack dynamic transformed into a new hierarchy. The most confident canine, the strongest of the new group, ascended to the alpha position, a communication primarily through energy, but sometimes the hierarchy was contested and determined through a brief scuffle.

One overweight female Chihuahua became the alpha of all forty-three survivors. One indicator that she was the alpha was her overprotection of the food, biting any other dog coming near it. We had to separate her from the others because she refused to allow them to eat; also, for her own good, we removed her from the food due to her obesity.

The best part of this experience was the disposition of the pups. Within just a few days, every pup became a pet. The property owner and his father were convicted of animal cruelty and of lying to police, and both served jail time for the puppy mill plans that had spiraled out of control.

The concerned citizen providing the tip to police had probably saved these dogs' lives.

9
BAILEY VERSUS THE TEA KETTLE— AND EVERY OTHER NOISE

I believe this next story will answer a lot of questions about the strange dog behaviors and phobias manifested when your pet's insecurities go unaddressed. Households can become so unbearable that Fido ends up losing his forever home and ends up in a shelter where he never again gets adopted because he is a mess.

I received a phone call from a delightful lady I knew because of her lovely volunteer work at my local animal shelter. She was good with dogs, and I was surprised when she related problems at home with her three-year old Corgi.

She was regularly getting bitten by her own pet.

Upon my arrival, Bailey the Corgi barked at me; he was a bit excitable, but to be honest, not too threatening. When I corrected him, he seemed to take it well. Right away, Bailey and I took a short walk with the red leash. The walk went so well, I wondered what I was doing there, until I sat down at the kitchen table with his owners and they described their living nightmare. Apparently, every normal household noise set Bailey off: the teakettle, the telephone, and the washing machine—even the creaking of the basement door. A sudden noise sent Bailey into a tailspin, and when the easygoing owners tried to calm the overstimulated dog down, he bit them. Their admission amazed me. You couldn't have met a sweeter couple, and it was becoming clear to me that this pleasantness was possibly the problem: there was no powerful, alpha human in the home. Thus, as dogs will do, Bailey thought it necessary to step up to the alpha position. And, like always, when dogs attempt to alpha over humans, they get into trouble because it just won't work. What happened to Bailey was that there was so much anxiety in trying to do a job that he was unable to do, he had developed control issues.

This manifestation was no one's fault, it was just a result of circumstance. I mean, if you threw a Master Plumber into a hospital and told him he had no choice but to operate on human beings, how long would it take for the plumber to break down? In my opinion, this was Bailey's case.

The fix? I explained to these nice people, was uncomplicated but required a little patience and a lot of commitment. We began by keeping Bailey tethered to me with the red leash and then set the tea kettle to boil.

When the kettle whistled, I gave Bailey a correction, a light snap of the red leash high behind his ears. The correction not only distracted him from the noise but also told him I disapproved of this bad behavior. The trick was to correct him before he completely went off; in other words, I wanted to nip it in the bud. Bailey accepted the correction and dealt with the teakettle. He really did well because he received what he had been lacking and craving—direction.

Remember the formula: when alpha wolf gives direction, the pack feels secure; when the pack feels secure, the pack feels safe; and when the pack feels safe—they, and you, are happy.

I needed to explain to Bailey's owners: Bailey was a very unhappy dog. If they wanted Bailey to be happy and for all his problems to go away, they needed to take charge with a strong, powerful alpha manner.

They needed to give Bailey direction.

Later, we followed through with the dishwasher, telephone, clothes washer and dryer (including the alarm), can opener, and even the creaky cellar door. Bailey did great if the red leash correction came at Bailey's first notice of the noise rather than in the middle of his hissy fit.

Although Bailey's behavior was extreme and dangerous, the cause was not uncommon. I see this lack of direction cause problems all the time. Humans like to label it as "He is just dumb," or, "He must have had something happen to him when he was young." Remember, dogs live in the now; they forget about their past. That's not to say dogs don't have scars or carry damage, but they just don't dwell on it, and they don't recall it. While they are affected by the past, they never live in it; they live in the now.

My mantra? Focus on the situation at hand. If there is a problem, identify it. If you want the problem to go away, let the dog know through direction. They will not take exception or get their feelings hurt. They will thank you. When a dog chases his tail or chews on himself or licks too much, correct it. He will thank you. A dog never wants to live with anxieties and phobias and needs your help getting past them with direction and correction. Be a strong alpha and help them. Remember, two words that are not in a dog's vocabulary: sympathy and empathy. Don't ever feel badly or waste your time trying to understand the behaviors of a dog. Simply correct it and direct it. That is the best thing you can do, rather than proffering chewy bones or furry toys or a soft bed.

It's about direction!

At my last follow up visit with Bailey he was doing well, and, according to his owners, "Bailey is a happy guy!"

Another recent example of out-of-control behavior rooted in fear and anxiety was a call from a gentleman in an adjacent county. He wanted my thoughts about his English Bulldog, who had been calm until recently. The dog had become aggressive and had also started biting. The owner feared an escalation resulting in a need to put his beloved dog down.

English Bulldogs are well known for being very stubborn.

In fact, English Bulldogs were bred to be fearless and to latch on to the leg of a bull or cow and not let go. This is why they were chosen for the United States Marine Corp mascot. Interestingly, the name of the dog I was consulted to control was Gunner.

Upon arriving at the home, I was surprised at the dynamic of the family. The caller, a dad in his forties, had two sons, one fifteen and the other seventeen years old. All of these men were quite tall. As I've established, I stand well over six feet tall, and all of these guys stood at least my height or larger, and each weighed an average of about three hundred pounds of pure muscle. Their girth made even more sense to me why this household kept an English Bulldog for a pet. The mother of the man was slight and pretty for a matron in her sixties. She was no bigger than a minute, but who do you think was the only human alpha in the house? It was she, the tiny, slender grandma.

After this clear understanding of the family dynamic, I walked Gunner. He was a perfect gentleman, so well-behaved that, upon returning to the house, I jokingly asked why they had summoned me.

The oldest son showed me on his left hand the holes inflicted by Gunner. The stories about Gunner continued, revealing the problem: Gunner was afraid of almost everything, anything new, such as a box on the floor or any sudden, unusual noise outside. Grandma had no problems with Gunner because she never tolerated his phobias, never failing to correct him when he acted out from his fears.

The men of the house seemed to have missed this cue. When nervous Gunner was startled, he attempted to correct the family with a reactionary bite. My job at this point was to explain that Gunner was not aggressive, just nervous. I suggested the family needed to heal the dog's nerves, and I taught the teenage boys to step up like alphas and to correct Gunner—that everyone needed to correct these phobias in order to make Gunner feel more secure. Only then would he stop biting them.

I realized this family would be successful, because they were dedicated— and because they had Grandma!

Both stories demonstrate the misbehavior of a dog transitioning either from secure to insecure or from insecure to secure. These problems are rectified with the solid leadership of a human alpha.

10
BEAR AND FOOD AGGRESSION

If you observe the world of wild canines (wolves, coyotes, foxes, hyenas and wild dogs), you will almost always see some degree of food aggression. It's my opinion that all of these creatures have at some time in their lives suffered starvation. Whether wild or stray, a meal is seldom handed over, and therefore, hunger is not uncommon. A lot of dogs in local shelters suffered food deprivation before arriving at the shelter, and therefore food-aggressive behavior of an abandoned or stray dog is never surprising.

This lack of security from wondering where the next meal is coming from creates this damaged behavior. They are not thinking about their pasts, yet they can be acutely damaged by their past. There is a difference. In time, and with rehabilitation, this problem can be resolved when they feel secure about their next provenance. The problem is that the first meeting of a dog and a potential adopter is so important, and no one wants to adopt a dog likely to devour fingers too close to the food bowl. Parents worry about small children, particularly, wandering over to the dish.

This was the scenario with Bear, a handsome brown and black, hundred-plus pound Rottweiler. Bear was the shelter-given name: he was a stray and had to be trapped due to fear he would never come quietly. As frightful as it was for us to capture Bear, imagine how frightened he was being taken down with a rabies pole, the six foot metal contraption officers use to wrangle hard-to-handle or vicious animals. The wire noose at the end of it adjusts around the animal's neck. No one knew anything about Bear; we surmised someone had just dumped him on a country road, leaving him to fend for himself. It seems incomprehensible that someone would do such a thing to him, but abandonment of dogs seems increasingly common. Some admit doing this believing a stranger will pity the dog and take it in, while others are unwilling to pay the fee for surrendering a dog to a shelter, oblivious of the consequences, such as many potential pets hit by cars, injured in the wild, or dead by starvation. What's more, delivering a poor creature to a shelter assures less likelihood of learning behaviors inhibiting the ability to find a home.

When a stray is brought to the shelter, poor behavior from the caged dog is never uncommon, because, after all, he doesn't know you and has no reason to trust you. He is stuck in the flight or fight mindset. He can't run anywhere, and therefore behaves like a nut.

This was not Bear's case, however. Although he was a bit scary, he seemed to settle down quickly. After a short session sitting next to Bear's cage on my upside down, blue plastic, five-gallon bucket while letting him get a nose full of my scent, we were off for a nice walk using the red leash. Bear already knew his basic commands of "sit," "come," "heel," and "stay," so I sensed we would get along fine.

After our walk, I neared his food bowl to fill it, and my gentle Bear turned into Angry Grizzly Bear. I nearly had to count my fingers afterwards. I pondered how we would ever adopt out this gentle giant gone Cujo on us. I knew Bear was too valuable and had too much potential not to give him a chance at rehab. Indeed, I took Bear home for six days of food aggression rehabilitation.

When it was mealtime at home, the first thing I did was to remove all other dogs from the house so that Bear and I were alone. I kept the energy low and did nothing to telegraph to Bear that it was mealtime. I ran my hands through the food, leaving my scent all over it. My aim was to let Bear know that this food was my food—not his—and that I was merely sharing it with him.

The mistake many people make when feeding their dog is raising the energy level at suppertime, asking excitedly, "Are you hungry?"and, "Are you a good boy?" shaking the bag of food and creating other dinnertime rituals that unnecessarily raise the dog's excitement level.

Then what does Fido do? Watch, he will stand over the bowl, claiming it. And the moment he claims that bowl of food, you could have a serious problem.

After loading my scent in Bear's food, I sat holding the bowl and fed him one piece at a time. Again, this is not his food; it's my food, I am only letting him have some. After proving to me that he can nibble pieces of kibble gently from my hands, and not until then, I can let him start taking food from the bowl, while I am still holding the bowl. If he tries to eat fast or aggressively, I pull the bowl away and make him sit, and we start the ritual all over again with the hand feeding. Only when I see him relax while eating do I try to place the food on the floor.

If you believe you are ready to place the bowl down on the floor, be sure that there is only a little food left in the bowl, maybe fifteen pieces. If he tries to hover over the bowl and claim it, carefully take it away. Use a broomstick or something similar to slide the bowl away from him. Repeat this ritual for several days, and when your pet has learned to trust and not claim, your problem should subside.

You must keep in mind that this works only in a one dog home. If you have more than one dog, and one of them is food aggressive, that food aggressive dog may learn to trust you, but that never means he or she will trust the other pack members. Feed the food aggressive pack members separately.

After six days, Bear seemed to become his trusting old self, but that didn't mean all was well. Unfortunately, Bear was adopted too quickly for effective follow through rehabilitation.

Bear had been adopted by a nice lady who already had a female Rottweiler. Both dogs got along great. The lady always fed the dogs separately, and Bear behaved well at dinnertime. One careless moment changed everything. The lady innocently treated herself to a bowl of ice cream while watching television. Both dogs were watching her eat and, suddenly, it was like flicking on a light switch. The lady did not realize that Mother Nature had kicked in, activating the salivary glands and changing the dog's state of mind. Insecurity took over and ignited an incident. Bear attacked the female Rottweiler, starting a bloody fight. The next day, Bear was surrendered back to the shelter. Sadly, this occurred because of a careless mistake. Bear trusted the lady, but he did not trust the other dog.

There is a happy ending to this story: Bear was adopted again, this time to a gentleman who lived alone and had no other dogs. Bear lived out the rest of his life happy and trusting with his new best friend.

The three most problematic behaviors I tend to work with that can be dangerous or destructive are: food aggression, dog aggression, and separation anxiety. I find food aggression the easiest to work with and to rehabilitate, requiring patience but mostly just commitment. You simply need to let your dog know you are alpha, and nothing is his to claim—not the furniture, not the food.

11
STAR'S TROUBLES IN THE BARN

One day, strolling through our local animal shelter, I encountered the most beautiful red and white Husky. Her name was Star. On the kennel door was a tag declaring that Star was being held by court order, possibly to be put down. Further investigation revealed that Star had been allowed to wander too far from her owner while visiting a friend, and trouble had ensued.

The next lesson is important: always know the whereabouts of your pet, particularly if you are on foreign turf. Pets are likely to find trouble when removed from the influence of your alpha energy and left alone to make their own decisions.

Bottom line: unfamiliar surroundings may minimize careful training.

While Star was on her adventure walk, she saw a cow barn at a neighboring farm and sauntered inside and over to a corral with several calves. Star's primitive, predatory instincts took over, and all hell broke loose. When the chaos was over, four calves were severely injured, one fatally.

When I heard that the court would probably euthanize Star, I asked to attend the court session and to offer my services to rehabilitate Star if the owner was willing to cooperate.

It was clear to the court that the young lady owning Star was deeply sorry for the barn incident and that her love for Star was sincere. Although deeming Star dangerous, the court graciously declared it unnecessary to put Star down, at least not yet. A New York court's "dangerous" verdict, however, creates quite a burden on the pet owner: the pet must be under the owner's personal control 24 hours a day, seven days a week. The pet must also have an indoor and outdoor kennel and must always wear a muzzle while outside. A chain, an outside run, or left alone are all unacceptable and, in Star's case, the dog and owner must have at least four training sessions with me.

This case was going to be interesting, because I was clearly going to battle Mother Nature. Mother Nature does not like to lose and has a powerful edge on her side. Star was only doing what her breed was built for—she was put on earth not only to pull a sled but to hunt. She had no idea she was doing anything wrong. Teaching her (or any other dog) to act differently is entirely the owner's responsibility—and I was honored to be helping.

When I arrive at a home, I always ask the owner not to restrain or hold back the dog. It's important that I start evaluating from the first impression. If a dog greets me in a rude manner—by jumping, by barking excessively, or by growling, I want the opportunity to correct the behavior. First of all, I must stress to the pet the misbehavior. Secondly, I must establish myself as the alpha character within the first five or ten minutes after arriving.

When Star greeted me at the door, she was very friendly, in fact, too friendly. Keep in mind that Star and I had met at the shelter and had even walked together, but this was a new scenario in a different environment. She was welcoming me for the first time on her territory. When she jumped on me, I hissed at her loudly and pushed my palm toward her face.

You know how it feels when someone stands too close to you, violating your personal space? By pushing energy from my hand toward Star's face, I was doing the same thing. Because dogs are one hundred times more sensitive than we are, this hand motion makes them uncomfortable. It constitutes the correction, and this correction shocked her. I placed the red leash on her immediately, high behind the ears, and we went for a walk.

Another reason I knew this case was something worthy of my time was that I was going to teach a husky to walk in the heel position, despite the fact that her instinct tells her that she was put on earth to pull and to hunt.

To be sure, this is rather like Albert Einstein's statement: "Don't expect a fish to climb a tree."

Star did want to pull like a dog on a sled team, but with an extra dose of dominant alpha attitude from me, Star decided within just a few minutes to cooperate.

Star's owner and I discussed the training. She lacked an understanding of Star's need to be controlled, but this young lady was so dedicated, I knew Star was in good hands. Because of that, I taught her and other human pack members how to understand and how to control Star. Ultimately, they were all positive and helpful in Star's rehabilitation.

Our second biggest challenge became convincing Star she did not need to be the predator she believed herself to be. She had absolutely no idea there was anything wrong with hunting those calves, thinking no different from my Labrador Retriever, who certainly didn't believe there was anything wrong with killing and retrieving the pheasant we were hunting one year.

My tactic to teach Star a new way of thinking? I decided to return her and her owner to the scene of the crime.

Approaching the barn, Star became excited. She received her first red leash correction. I didn't want to wait until she got so excited that there was no turning back, and therefore her excitement had to be cut off immediately.

Making the situation even more challenging, both the inside and outside of the barn were loaded with cats. Cats in or around a barn are pretty common, but there were at least thirty of them. Needless to say, Star was getting her share of corrections. Proceeding through the adult cow portion of the barn and into the calf section, Star became overwhelmed. She was confused, shaking, and whining a lot. The calves seemed more curious than frightened.

Each time Star became excited, she received a correction and was forced to sit with her back facing the livestock; eventually, she was forced to lie down inside the corral, within inches of the calves, and to lie submissively until she relaxed. This session and technique took less than an hour, but I could see it had profoundly affected the dog. We repeated the technique during our final session. This time, I watched Star's young owner walking her pet past the cats and into the calf corral. Star passed with flying colors by staying among the calves for a much longer time without any need for correction.

The even better news? The court was gracious enough to lift the muzzle restriction and offered to review the case later in hope that Star would no longer be deemed dangerous!

This story has many lessons: Understand your dog. Understand the breed. Any dog can find trouble if you let it run unmonitored or uncontrolled. Train your dog to be the dog you want. Star was a very sweet animal, but unmonitored she was a killer—through no fault of her own.

12
THE KINDNESS
OF STRANGERS

In July 2014, a young lady in a van traveled a dark country road around two in the morning, and on a small knoll her headlights highlighted an ocean of reflecting eyes. A herd of deer, she thought initially, and jammed the brakes hard in hopes of avoiding a collision, but then came clarity and surprise. She stared at fifteen dogs in two wire cages, placed not on the shoulder, but right smack in the middle of the road. One cage held puppies approximately six weeks old. The second cage contained older puppies crowded like sardines in a can. One larger adult male, approximately two years old, was tied outside. One adult dog ran loose outside the cages, circling them excitedly, as though trying to summon help from the woman. But when the vehicle pulled up, the free dog suddenly scuttled into the bushes alongside the ditch.

What happened next still amazes me: this wonderful, brave woman collected fourteen of the fifteen dogs and placed them into the van. When she reached to slide shut the side door, Mr. Fifteen, to avoid separation from his pack, dashed madly to the closing door and jumped in. Within hours, all fifteen were delivered to the county animal shelter and were safely ensconced in kennels for the night—except elusive Mr. Fifteen, who had finally decided to escape into the darkness. But when the sun came up, he waited at the shelter door, wanting his pack. He refused to be touched, leashed, or handled in any way. The animal control officer opened the shelter door for him, and he rushed in. When she tried to leash him, he lunged at her. She was unhurt and happily stated, "At least we got him inside!" She let him hide in the grooming room a while and eventually maneuvered him into a kennel with a rabies pole.

The second day of our new adventure consisted of evaluating the health and temperament of our new visitors and trying to determine why this event had transpired. The dogs had been discovered about thirty miles from the Pennsylvania/ New York state line. The New York State Police had noticed a pickup truck with a Pennsylvania registration but had had no reason to suspect anything amiss. We decided this tragedy was another puppy mill gone awry. Some people think a puppy mill is an easy way to make money until it soon gets out of control.

The six puppies were adorable and were readily adopted, but the remainder of the pack were a challenge. All the dogs appeared to be black Labrador Retrievers, but they clearly weren't pedigreed. The remaining dogs, seven yearlings, a two-year-old, and mercurial Mr. Fifteen, were all terrified of the red leash. The moment we tried to place a leash on them, they panicked, requiring days of patient training and reassurance to relax the yearlings into accepting any direction. Proving the goodness of people, I can happily boast that all seven puppies landed in superb forever homes. Better still, not one of them came back.

An old friend of mine from Buffalo saw the story on television and became interested in the two year old, whom we had named Henley. I had tried to lead him from his kennel with a red leash. Although I was gentle, Henley panicked, biting the lead so violently that he injured his mouth. He was bleeding, and so I released the leash and, of course, he ran into the grooming room. There was something about that room! It took a couple of hours, but Henley eventually let me sit beside him on the floor and lightly stroke his forehead. I was intensely focused on Henley when I heard someone say, "Hey, Thomas, what are you doing here?"

It was my old friend Hank from Buffalo.

I invited him to join the Henley love fest. To my delight, Henley accepted Hank. I left Henley with Hank and his wife for about ten minutes. Upon my return, Hank said he and his wife were sure they wanted to adopt Henley when he was ready. They had perfect energy, and a month later Henley, whose new name was Moses, was ready and moved to his forever home.

On a follow up call, I asked Hank how Moses made out with housebreaking. Hank said the only accident occurred when Hank's infant granddaughter waddled toward the dog with both arms flailing, freaking Moses out because he had no idea how to respond, and he pooped—understandable, and no cause for concern.

Fierce Mr. Fifteen was so damaged, it took a week to just touch him, and that was done very carefully. Someone nicknamed him "Grumpy" because all he did was show his teeth and growl. I heard it said more than once that he probably should be put down. I spent many hours sitting in Mr. Fifteen's cage with him, filling him with my scent and with my calm energy before ever trying to leash him. This process took two weeks before he finally allowed me to escort him out of the cage on a leash. Most of my time I spent focused on him, although all the dogs had issues, just less severe. All of them suffered meltdowns when confronted with a red leash.

Frequently, I found a volunteer named Jean singing "You Are My Sunshine" softly and soothingly outside of Grumpy's kennel. She claimed it was his favorite song because it visibly settled him down. We soon changed his name to Luke because "Grumpy" just seemed too negative, and he had enough going against him already.

Sadly, statistics tell us seventy percent of dogs entering a U.S. shelter are euthanized. Only under the guidance of volunteers like Jean or Animal Control officers such as Justa Goodell would a dog like Luke ever have had a chance at a happy life. At one point, Luke was adopted by a good family, but it didn't work out, because Luke was a special needs dog, and the energy in the home was just too much for him to handle. Luke's slow-mending fear of people was one of my larger projects. I withdrew Luke from the shelter frequently in attempts to socialize him, scheduling car rides, boat rides, walks in parks, bonfires, even walking without a leash. He progressed to a point, but unfortunately, caged in the kennel that long for nearly a year had taken its toll. Very unhappy, he developed hotspots on his legs and paws and messed his own kennel.

And so, I did it—I broke my biggest rule, but with the blessing of my wife, we adopted Luke.

It's hard to believe even to this day. Although Luke still has challenging moments, he became best friends with Carley, my Labrador/Weimaraner mix, and he heels better than any other pup I know. I have been trying to teach Luke to pheasant hunt with Carley, but Carley hunts birds; Luke usually hunts me.

13
YOUR TURN?

I want to start by declaring to all of you who kindly and bravely rescued your pet from the shelter: you are true heroes, and I love you. The decision to adopt is hard enough, but the adjustment period afterwards can be incredibly trying, requiring a commitment to get through some of the bumps along the road.

The benefits, however? Well, they nearly always exceed the sacrifice.

I have been blessed the last few years volunteering at the Wyoming County Animal Shelter in Wyoming County, New York. The person in charge there is the closest thing to an angel that I have ever met: Animal Control Officer Justa Goodell, one of those 24/7 employees rightfully credited with some astounding statistics.

I mentioned previously that approximately seventy percent of dogs brought to U.S. animal shelters are euthanized. My observations at the Wyoming Shelter place that number at five percent or less, usually sick animals or court orders. Justa has an amazing knack for getting these guys adopted. I have heard it said that she is a great used dog salesman. Indeed, I am grateful for everything she has taught me thus far, and I hope she keeps this old dog around for a long time.

If you decide on a shelter, whether in response to an online posting or because it's where you want to start searching for your forever pet, stay open- minded and patient. Don't rush into any decisions. The first behavior you witness from these creatures may be very misleading.

Yes, first impressions can be false.

If you approach a kennel and the canine inside behaves like a lunatic, don't automatically dismiss that animal. He may just be exhibiting signs of fight or flight syndrome. In this situation, any creature, human or animal, must decide if it feels trapped. Either I stay (fight), or I run away (flight). The decision is usually deep and visceral with little thought—a primal, instinctual reaction if you will. If the dog you approach is nervous and unable to run away because it's trapped in a cage, the creature has no choice but to try to scare you from hurting it. Ask the individual in charge to take the pet out of the cage.

The first time I approach a dog in a kennel, I approach slowly and sideways. I also grab a five-gallon water bucket, turn it upside down, and sit on it near the cage door, my shoulder to the kennel so that the dog can get more than enough of my scent. If through scent he detects that I am calm and not nervous, the dog will respond in kind and also be calm.

I take my time before opening the kennel door and approaching the animal, again sideways, as this human behavior is less threatening. It's funny how the second you get the red leash on the dog, the whole game changes. Suddenly, the dog feels okay, there's no threat, and he wants to go for a walk. Once I get the dog outside, I heel him immediately. I want the dog to feel safe, and so I alpha all over him.

There is never any hurry in making your adoption decision. Nearly all shelters will allow you to put a hold on a dog so you can go home, have a family conference, and sleep on the matter. It's a big decision, and you'll know if it's the right one if you take your time. It's only fair to you, to your family, and to the dog to make a carefully considered decision.

The first dog I rescued from an SPCA was the Brittany Collie mix named Kelly I told you about at the beginning of this book. I still miss her. After I met her and thought I might want her, I went home, picked up my then six year old daughter, and returned, praying my daughter would gravitate toward her. She did just that, and soon Kelly had her forever home with us. It was important for not just me but my daughter, too, to feel that Kelly was the right dog.

I'd like to tell you another quick story about first impressions. I visited the shelter one day, and Justa introduced me to the biggest Red Nose Pit Bull I had ever seen. His name was Gator, and with the size of his teeth the name was appropriate. When I approached the outdoor cage, Gator lunged at me, smashing into the door of the cage, scaring the life out of me. Justa approached the cage in the same manner and Gator lunged at her, too, snarling viciously. We were uncertain how to proceed and decided on an experiment, something we do frequently at the shelter.

Justa approached the cage again at the front, while I crept to the rear. When Gator sprang at Justa, I shouted, "Hey!" and the dog stopped and glared at me. I commanded him to come, thereby giving him direction. He came to me, and I told him to sit, and he did. Suddenly, he was calm, and I decided to trust him, trusting the theory that there is no reason for a dog to trust you, if you do not trust him. I will admit I was still a bit nervous, but it was time to take Gator for a walk on the red leash. I asked the other people present to keep a watchful eye on Gator in case I needed their help, but the walk went great, and Gator and I became very good friends.

It is immaterial if you are dealing with a three-pound Chihuahua or with a one hundred-and-twenty-pound pit bull named Gator—fear is universal, and very traumatizing for all dogs.

Gator had nowhere to run, didn't know us, and wondered if we were going to hurt him, and so he chose to fight. Understandable. Once he heard solid, firm commands, however, he felt safer and therefore able to respond. I knew that Gator was unadoptable until he gained some confidence, and I worked hard with him, even taking him home for days at a time to socialize him. Gator did get adopted by a U.S. Customs agent and is now down on the Arizona/Mexico border, hopefully enjoying a great life.

Another helpful virtue while investigating your local shelter is patience. Though I don't want you entering feeling sorry for these critters, I do want you to have an open heart. You will find dogs with special needs, and you might just be the special person for them. We had an abandoned stray come to our shelter, a ninety-pound white American Bulldog we named Toby. The first time I took Toby out of his kennel, I was nearly mauled, contending with pure muscle. I was unsure who was in charge. Poor Toby knew nothing: not sit, not to stay, not to come; nothing. One of Toby's rudest habits was mouthing. He wasn't biting, but he was hurting us without realizing it. Mouthing is a puppy trait, but if uncorrected, becomes a dominance behavior. We also noticed that when Toby was asleep, he didn't hear us call his name. A check with the veterinarian confirmed that Toby was deaf. We had our work cut out for us; Toby was a guest at the shelter for almost a year.

One afternoon, while teaching Toby manners and hand signals, a veritable band of angels appeared: a Mom, Dad, and a sweet ten year-old girl came in and fell for Toby. They took their time to make any decision to see if they could work with Toby, and they finally adopted him, displaying one of the most moving love affairs you would ever hope to witness. I have seen our wild child since; he is calm, happy, and very well-behaved. His family walks Toby all over town, and you would never know he was handicapped or different from other dogs in any way.

Once you decide on your forever pet, how do you proceed? After you and your new pet arrive at Fido's new home, your first step is to, yep, take that red leash and walk around the neighborhood. If potty is called for, that's fine, but marking every object approached needs to be corrected. Dogs test the limitations, much like a horse trying to eat grass the second you are on his back. After the walk, introduce the dog to the home. Most people merely open the door and let the dog run in freely to check out his new home; a huge mistake, if allowed to run free inside this cozy new environment with dog bowls and fluffy, comfortable furniture and beds, the dog might claim the place and everything in it as his or her own, creating a huge problem down the road. Here's my rule: Until your new dog pays the mortgage or rent, nothing is his!

Let's return to the front door with our new family member. First step is to sit him at the entrance, requiring a little patience on your part. Now, with one end of the leash on your puppy and the other end of the leash on your hand, open the front door and slowly try to enter the house while Fido remains sitting in place just outside the door. If he attempts to enter before being invited, repeat the exercise until he gets it.

Just because a door is open doesn't mean he gets to pass through it.

When he does get it and remains sitting outside while you are inside, you are ready to invite him in. Do this as calmly as you can, as you don't yet want to raise his energy level. I strongly suggest you repeat this ritual at every threshold in the house, and after briefly entering each room, escort him around it, but don't linger. A quick introduction to each room is all you need to claim each room. When this exercise is complete, you have claimed your entire house with a technique that saves you the frustration of Fido (especially males) marking his new territory. Please understand that this "each room" ritual should be a one-time thing, not so true with entering and leaving the house; you should always, without exception, enter the outdoors before your pet, claiming the outdoors for yourself rather than for your pet. The same with your home, always entering it first while Fido waits outside until he is invited inside.

Let's discuss furniture and beds. Do you want your pet to sleep with you? That's fine, but there must be a simple rule: he or she is never allowed to jump up on the bed until invited. If your pet makes the decision about when to enter the bed, the dog will claim this bed, and you also risk Fido claiming you—presenting a big problem if you share, or may eventually share, the bed with another human. I have heard many times that after your pet claims you, it is not uncommon to mark the other mate's side of the bed with urine or with a nice big poop, indicating serious problems when your new significant other begins spending the night or moves in.

Another frequent problem is puppies claiming a piece of furniture. Never allow the pet on any furniture unless invited. If on the couch, lead the dog off it with the red leash. The red leash expresses and represents correction. And again, leading the dog off the furniture is more natural; you wouldn't push a horse from behind, or you might get kicked, and a pushed dog may bite. Leading is far more natural, and the dog won't fight it. Just a reminder: nothing in the house belongs to the dog, not even the dog food. Your pet, as a new home addition, will never resent your guidance, rather, as I emphasize throughout this book, he will welcome it.

When you are assertive and strong, puppy feels safe and happy.

If your new pet does have an accident in the home, grab a newspaper, roll it up very tightly, and hit yourself in the head with it because you probably weren't paying attention, and so it was probably your fault.

Some of the shelter dogs I met and worked with will stay in my heart forever, unforgettable dogs like Lance. We found Lance lying in a ditch, emaciated and mostly dead, but what a spirit this guy had. Through his recovery, we became very close. He was one of the most balanced dogs I believe I had ever encountered. If I had to deal with a questionable or vicious dog, I used Lance every time. This Pit/Lab mix would walk up to the cage of a nervous dog and and calm him down immediately. The communication was subtle, hardly discernible, but intensely powerful.

I used Lance to help me with dozens of dogs, and I strongly considered taking him home, but a senior lady came in and declared Lance was going home with her. I wondered how this lovely elder would be able to handle Lance, especially when I found out she already had two other dogs. This couldn't end well, I thought. Ask me how the crow tasted, because that is exactly what I had to eat—I was wrong. I visited Lance at his new home and had never seen a happier dog. The lady was calm and quiet but assertive alpha, very direct with her animals, exactly like Lance himself—their personalities were a perfect match.

If you do head to the shelter to scout out a new dog, be sure you are in the proper mindset. I once noticed a burly hulk of a man wandering around the shelter for about four days. I thought him a volunteer until he walked up to me and asked how he could become a volunteer. He was considering adopting a rescue and said, "Even though I'm a large burly guy, these dogs make me want to cry." I didn't want to be harsh but advised him that he probably should not be here, especially if he was thinking about adopting. He would just be asking for trouble. I advised him that if he adopted a dog in his present state of mind, he was probably taking home a nightmare. You should never feel sorry for a dog. We humans mistake feeling sorry for caring; dogs see feeling sorry as a weakness, and the last thing they need is a weak human. If I am perceived by a dog to be weak, the dog's first reaction is to step up to the alpha position; it's in his DNA, and the problems begin. So, if you decide to pet "shop" at your local shelter, head in with a stiff dose of attitude. That's what these pups need, never empathy or sympathy—just strong leadership.

At the beginning of this book I wrote that I simply do not believe dogs possess a soul. What I do feel however is something intensely spiritual behind their eyes.

Search for whatever this is, and look deep—because it is there. Communicate to your dog without using words. You will capture the light I allude to, and you will connect to that spiritual energy. And know, it is worth the wait to find it—because the human/animal relationship can be the most indelible experience of your life.

We all feel the kinship to the species already. Nothing else will open a conversation like discussing someone's pet. When I converse with someone and the person learns I am a dog trainer, there is no escape; the direction of the conversation has now been set in stone.

It is without question that I have been truly blessed. Of all my life's adventures, nothing has taught me more or has been more fulfilling than learning the beautiful art of dogs, that tender universal yearning for unconditional trust and love. There is so much reciprocal warmth and nurturing: what we give is dwarfed by what we receive in return. I truly hope this book has provided you direction for fulfilling your relationship with your dog.

We hear over and over again in the popular culture that they are man's best friend—but we all know they are much more than that.

The millions of our four-legged friends deserving and needing our help will never go away. The torrent of animals needing homes and love and direction is unstoppable and unending. If we do our best to do the humane thing, however, we can curb a lot of the pain and suffering.

Just think with your brain and not with your heart; take on no more than you can handle. Don't rescue four dogs if your environment is unequipped to handle four dogs. Be smart, and be practical.

It has been a privilege sharing my experiences with you; but alas, I have two sets of patient but imploring eyes staring up at me, conveying the message, "C'mon big guy, it's time for a walk."

Off we go!

CPSIA information can be obtained
at www.ICGtesting.com
Printed in the USA
FSOW01n1940261216
28864FS